7-19-62

Ministries of Mercy

❧❧

Ministries of Mercy

by

FERN BABCOCK GRANT

1192099

Contents

CONTENTS

CONTENTS

CHAPTER ONE

Why Christians Minister to Persons in Need

. . . as you did it to one of the least of these my brethren, you did it to me. —Matthew 25:40.

When ten-year-old Peter came to live at the Church Home for Boys, hate was the only emotion he had ever experienced. His mother had deserted the family when he was a baby. His father, who was an alcoholic, beat him frequently. When the caseworker tried to help him, Peter shouted, "I hate you. I hate God!" The caseworker did not tell him that it was a sin to hate; nor did he tell him that God felt a Father's love for him. These Christian truths would have had no meaning for Peter. Instead the caseworker began a long series of interviews with the boy, during which he accepted Peter's anger and absorbed some of his hostility. Intelligent, loving guidance gradually released Peter from bondage to hate and he became a normal boy.

Mr. Matthews was almost too old to live alone, but he did not want to go East to live with his son. He loved to be independent; to work in his garden and to visit with old friends. But most of all he enjoyed participation in the life of Grace Church, where he and Mrs. Matthews had been members for more than fifty years. Now that she was gone, the church was the center of his life. When he became too feeble to cook his own meals, the Social Service Committee of the church found volunteers to take a hot meal to him each day and to visit him in the evenings. When he died in his sleep one night, the visitor who found his body was shocked that he had been alone when death came. But other members of the congregation knew that he had been able to live his last years as he wished—in his own home, among the friends of a lifetime, and as an active member of his church.

Ruth was a sophomore in college when she realized that she was to have a child out of wedlock. She sought help from the maternity service of her denomination and was placed with a family in another city. The caseworker and the members of the family treated her with kindness and respect. She attended church services and took communion during the months of her pregnancy. She decided that she would release the baby for adoption and enter another college to continue her training as a chemist. A healthy boy was born after a short and easy delivery. When the caseworker visited her in the hospital, Ruth was distraught and in tears. The poise and serenity that she had maintained during pregnancy were gone. The caseworker tried to discover the reasons for her anxiety. After searching for clues she found that Ruth was not disturbed because the baby was to be placed for adoption, but because she had sinned and had not been punished. Although the experience was nearly over, no one had condemned or punished her. The caseworker was able to help Ruth analyze these feelings and to accept the fact that God had forgiven her and that she was free to begin a new life.

Why were members of Grace Church glad to help Mr. Matthews spend the last year of his life in his own home? Why do churches employ highly skilled staff members who are ready to give expert help to unloved boys such as Peter, to unwed mothers such as Ruth, and to hundreds of thousands of other persons in need? Why do several million Christians respond to the needs of fellow church members every year? Why do the churches support hundreds of agencies and institutions that give aid and comfort to persons in distress? Why do church members give not only money but time in voluntary work with these organizations?

NOT ALL CHRISTIANS RESPOND

Before attempting to say why Christians help their neighbors who are in trouble, it is necessary to record that not all of them do! Many are able to close their eyes to the needs of their neighbors and to keep all that they have for themselves.

It is also necessary to add that some individuals of other faiths and of no faith respond more quickly and generously to requests for help than do many Christians. A number of the outstanding leaders in humanitarian causes are not members of a church or synagogue. Some of these persons may have learned their habits of giving from parents who were deeply religious, but they have not made that faith their own.

It is true, however, that giving is an integral part of the Christian religion and that church members have traditionally been in the forefront of those who have been concerned about meeting the needs of their fellow men who are in trouble.

REASONS FOR ASSISTING

Why do Christians minister to persons in need? As we look into our own motives and those of others we see several reasons why Christians help those who are in trouble. Not all the reasons are laudable. Perhaps each of us is moved by a different combination of motives as we respond to various situations. At times our giving may be for completely selfish reasons; at others it may be a spontaneous response to God's redemptive love in Christ. Among the reasons why Christians give help to others are these.

Giving is a natural response. Man was created by God in such a way that one response to need is to want to help. If he has food and sees a person who is hungry, he may be moved to share it with him. But a perversion of love, love centered on self, may overcome the impulse to give assistance. An individual's desire for his own security and comfort may become so strong that the impulse to give is inhibited and he leads a self-enclosed life. However, no one becomes so hardened, so self-centered, that he is not capable of feeling the impulse to help others.

Christians inherit a tradition of giving. Christianity grew out of Judaism and is indebted to it for a profound sense of the responsibility of every man for the well-being of his neighbors. The Jews remembered their years of slavery in Egypt and the fact that God had delivered them from bondage. They believed that rich and powerful persons had a responsibility to help the poor, the weak, the afflicted, and the oppressed. Since they were only stewards of God's property, they felt that they should use it for the welfare of all men. They considered it a duty to lend money without interest and to love their neighbors as themselves.

The early Christians inherited this tradition of responsibility for the well-being of neighbors from Judaism. According to Luke, the first public appearance of Jesus was in the temple, where he read these words from the book of Isaiah:

The Spirit of the Lord is upon me,
because he has anointed me to preach good news to the poor.
He has sent me to proclaim release to the captives
and recovering of sight to the blind,
to set at liberty those who are oppressed,
to proclaim the acceptable year of the Lord.

The New Testament records the many teachings of Jesus about giving to those in need and the response of the early church to this teaching.

The tradition of giving has been maintained throughout the long history of Christianity. Many Christians have grown up in homes where a certain amount of the family income was set aside for the church and for gifts to the needy. This custom has survived and is still widely practiced by Christians today.

Giving is an essential part of the Christian faith. Jesus made it abundantly clear that his mission was one of service and that his followers were also to be the servants of men. "The Son of Man came not to be served but to serve." "Not every one who says to me, 'Lord, Lord,' shall enter the kingdom of heaven, but he who does the will of my Father who is in heaven."

In his story of the last judgment, Jesus taught that service to the least of men was service to him. His words are given in Matt. 25:34-40:

Then the King will say to those at his right hand, "Come, O blessed of my Father, inherit the kingdom prepared for you from the foundation of the world; for I was hungry and you gave me food, I was thirsty and you gave me drink, I was a stranger and you welcomed me, I was naked and you clothed me, I was sick and you visited me, I was in prison and you came to me." Then the righteous will answer him, "Lord, when did we see thee hungry and feed thee, or thirsty and give thee drink? And when did we see thee a stranger and welcome thee, or naked and clothe thee? And when did we see thee sick or in prison and visit thee?" And the King will answer them, "Truly, I say to you, as you did it to one of the least of these my brethren, you did it to me."

Three central aspects of the life of the church as it is described in the New Testament are: *kerygma,* or the teaching and preaching of the good news of the gospel; *koinonia,* or the fellowship of the church in the presence of God; and *diakonia,* the expression of faith in love and service to all men. Each aspect exists in relation to the others; none can be omitted from the life of the Christian church. Neither a church nor a church member can be

Christian without participating in the ministry of love and service to others.

Giving brings recognition to the donor. The temptation to give so that one will be deemed generous is not new. Two thousand years ago, Jesus warned against this practice:

Thus, when you give alms, sound no trumpet before you, as the hypocrites do in the synagogues and in the streets, that they may be praised by men. Truly, I say to you, they have their reward.

The donor who seeks honor for himself by his gift may do much more harm than good. He not only detracts from the dignity of the receiver; he also infects the community with the virus of self-love.

Good works may be deemed payment for spiritual rewards. In the Roman Catholic Church of the Middle Ages, the forgiveness of sin was thought to be in proportion to one's giving to the church and to the needy. As St. John Chrysostom said, "If there were no poor the greater part of your sins would not be removed; they are the healers of our wounds." Although this concept is no longer taught in the churches, some Christians still try to buy their way into heaven by their gifts.

Giving contributes to the welfare of the donor. Much giving in the United States today is based on "enlightened self-interest." Christians maintain hospitals so that adequate facilities will be available when they are in need of them. They give money for research so that polio can be stamped out before it attacks their children. They build homes for the aging so that facilities will be available if they should ever need them. They work for better housing for low-income families so that slums will not rob the city of its beauty and security. They participate in many community projects so that their cities will be healthful, attractive places in which to live.

This reason for giving is not entirely selfish, even though self-interest looms as a large element in it. The motive of enlightened self-interest recognizes that all human beings are bound together in the bundle of life and that what affects one affects all. No one can meet the trials of life alone; by assisting one another we are also helping ourselves. Jesus recognized the validity of meeting one's own needs together with those of others when he made the self the norm in the second half of the great commandment, "Love your neighbor as yourself."

Giving is the response Christians make to the love of God. The fact that God became man through his Son, Jesus Christ, has given dignity and worth to every man. Therefore, the physical, mental, moral, and social welfare of every human being is of primary concern to the church. Each person must have the opportunity to become the person that God intended him to be. As John C. Bennett says:

God, as known to us through Christ, seeks a community that is favorable to the real welfare of all his children. What stands out most clearly as the social meaning of the New Testament teaching about God's purpose for man is that all groups of human beings are equally the objects of the love and concern of God. If there is inequality in the divine concern for men, it is the kind that undercuts all of our human schemes of inequality—it is God's special concern for the lost sheep, for those whom the world has discarded. . . . It means that all of the ways in which the privileged few have exploited and lorded it over the masses of men throughout history are an offense to God. It means that it is intolerable that there should be any persons, any groups of persons, who are the victims of policies or systems by which we profit or to which we consent. It means that every child has the same right as every other child to the conditions that are favorable to his development as a person, the right to be free from malnutrition, from the humiliation of racial discrimination and segregation, the right to have access to the means of health and education.[1]

No Christian can escape the divine imperative to do everything he can to make full and abundant life available to all men. Those who truly know the love of God will respond to him in love and service to their fellow men.

[1] Bennett, John C. *Christianity and Communism Today*, pp. 106-107. Association Press, 1960. Used by permission.

CHAPTER TWO

Religious Origins of Social Work

. . . you shall love your neighbor as yourself. —Leviticus 19:18.

For centuries, major responsibility for meeting the needs of the sick, the poor, the orphaned, and the widowed was carried by the churches. Within the last hundred years, much of this work has been assumed by private and government agencies. Today, the needs of more people are met by secular agencies and institutions than by those related to churches. However, many private and government agencies and institutions trace their origin to work begun by the churches. Many practices in social welfare were developed in church-related agencies. Religious faith motivates much secular welfare work today.

A review of the religious origins of social welfare work will clarify the current responsibilities of Christians.

PRIMITIVE SOCIETIES

Very little is known about the way hunting and gathering societies cared for the sick, the disabled, the aged, and others who could not keep up with the movements of the tribe. Probably they were given little care and met an early death. More is known about the practices of the peoples who earned their living by cultivating the soil and tending flocks. Three or more generations lived together in one extended family, which was also the major economic unit. The head of the family directed the work of all of its able-bodied members and arranged for the care of the young, the ill, and the disabled. In self-sustaining agrarian families there were many tasks that could be performed by children, by the aging, by those who were partially disabled, and even by persons who were mentally retarded or disturbed. They could carry water, wash clothes, garden, and tend the babies; therefore, caring for them was not a complete drain on the family. Work that is now done as "occupational therapy" was once a normal part of the family economy.

Medical treatment was frequently associated with religious ceremonies. The priests of primitive tribes were also medicine men who ministered to the spirit, mind, and body. As early as 4000 B.C., certain deities were thought to have healing power. The temples of Saturn, Hygeia, and others were used as resting places for patients under treatment and as schools for medical practitioners.

SOCIAL SERVICE PRACTICES
OF RELIGIOUS FAITHS

While the larger tribal family had been able to cope with the death of a parent, serious illness, disablement, or other disaster, it was impossible for the smaller, city-dwelling family to do so. It was necessary to call for help from outside the family. In most instances this cry was answered by the religious community—or not at all. Various faiths met the needs of persons for help in different ways. Let us look briefly at the social service practices of several major faiths:

Buddhism. The practice of charity was taught by Buddha. One of the Buddhist emperors of India was led by his faith to provide medical services for the people of his realm. The infirmaries of Buddhist monasteries were intended for the monks, but sometimes they accepted patients from the outside. The introduction of Buddhism into Ceylon and China led to the establishment of social services in those countries. Buddhist monks used to study medicine and practice it without charge, as a part of their ministry. In China, Buddhists established houses of refuge for the sick as early as the first century, A.D. In 1271 A.D., the Emperor Kublai Khan initiated a wide program of relief and social reform that included the setting up of nursing establishments.

Islam. The philanthropic spirit of the rulers and nobility of Islam led them to establish hospitals. The first Arab hospital was founded at Damascus in 707 and another was established in Baghdad in 792. The Sultan erected a great hospital in Cairo in 1283 that pioneered in the development of many new features. Among them were: special wards for dysentery cases, feverish patients, ophthalmic cases, the injured, and convalescents; story tellers and musicians to amuse the patients; an organized medical service with male and female nurses; storerooms, kitchens, a dispensary, an herb garden, a library, lecture rooms, and common rooms for the doctors. The hospital was open to all. The Sultan wrote, "I have founded this institution for kings and servants, for amirs and soldiers, for rich and poor, for free and bond, for men and women alike."

Judaism. Early in its history, Judaism recognized that the earth and everything in it belonged to God. The Jews knew that their property belonged to God and that they used it as his stewards. They did not forget that they had once been slaves in Egypt. Therefore, the rich and powerful had clearcut responsibilities for the poor, the weak, and the afflicted. "When you reap the harvest of your land, you shall not reap your field to its very border, neither shall you gather the gleanings after your harvest. And you shall not strip your vineyard bare . . . ; you shall leave them [the fallen grapes] for the poor and for the sojourner." Money was loaned to the poor without interest. Debts were remitted every seventh and fiftieth year. Every Jew was to love his neighbor as himself and the stranger was to be treated as a native, for "you were strangers in the land of Egypt."

From the time of the fall of Jerusalem, every Jewish community has been expected to have its charity overseers. Jews have been encouraged to give at least a tenth of their incomes to philanthropic causes. Numerous voluntary organizations have operated to care for the poor, the sick, and the homeless.

While Judaism has esteemed and cared for the poor, it

has not glorified poverty. It has no mendicant orders. Loss of independence was traditionally regarded as one of the greatest hardships connected with poverty. The code of Maimonides enumerated eight grades of donors to charity; the highest place was accorded to him who advanced funds to enable a poor man to support himself, and the second to him who gave in such a way that the donor did not know the recipient nor the receiver the giver.

From the arrival of the first Jews in the United States early in the seventeenth century until the end of the eighteenth century, charity was dispensed by the synagogues. Jews not only assisted the poor and sick within their own congregations, but responded to requests from others at home and abroad.

Early Christianity. Following the tradition of Judaism and the teaching of Jesus Christ, the early Christians regarded giving as a part of their religious observance. Individuals and families were expected to assist those in need —"Give to him who begs from you, and do not refuse him who would borrow from you."

Christians not only gave to those in need but established church funds for the poor. From the beginning of Christianity, members brought every week or month gifts that were given to the church leaders to be used for the poor and needy. The gifts were laid on the Lord's table and consecrated to God; the recipients, therefore, received them from the hand of God. The deacons were responsible for the distribution of the gifts, which were given to the sick, the poor, the infirm, the disabled, prisoners, widows, and orphans. The common meals (love or *agape* feasts) eaten by church members also helped to feed the poor. Each person brought what he could afford, but everyone ate what he needed.

When the need for charity increased about the middle of the fourth century, the congregational method of collection and distribution had to be expanded. The bishop of a diocese appointed a steward for each city or district; it was his responsibility to call upon each church in his area for greatly increased funds.

In 321 the Roman Emperor Constantine gave authority for the church to receive legacies. Many of the large gifts that were received were used to establish hospitals, hostels for travelers, and institutions that aided orphans, widows, the aged, the blind, cripples, and others. It was during this period that the conviction developed that helping the needy was of as much value to the giver as to the recipient. The church taught that one's sins were forgiven in proportion to the amount of one's gifts to charity.

The first charity hospital in Rome was founded by a deaconess, Fabriola, about 300 A.D. During the Middle Ages a great many hospitals were established; by 1540 more than 750 had been founded in England alone.

The Franciscans, Dominicans, Carmelites, and other mendicant orders rendered another kind of service to the poor and needy. Rather than living in large monasteries as did the Benedictines and others, the friars of the mendicant orders established themselves in the poorest parts of the towns and went to the homes of the sick and the destitute to serve them.

The monastic system of relief began to break down long before it was disrupted by the Reformation. When Henry VIII and Edward VI closed the monasteries of England, these institutions had already ceased to serve their original purpose. Not only had the monasteries used methods of distribution that were indiscriminate, but they had also diverted money contributed for relief of the poor and the sick to other clerical funds.

Roman Catholicism. The development of Roman Catholic charities in the United States was a direct outgrowth of the tide of immigration that reached its height between 1840 and 1870. The new immigrants crowded into cities that had inadequate sanitary facilities for such great numbers of people. As a result disastrous epidemics broke out and thousands of children were left orphaned and homeless. The city parishes struggled to care for these children, but there were too many of them for the slender resources of the churches. They appealed to the Sisters of Charity and to other orders of women, some of which originated in the United States and others that were units of orders that had been established earlier in Europe. These orders responded by establishing institutions that were a combination of boarding school, day school, and orphanage. The church was concerned that orphans be reared not only in the faith but also in the customs of their parents. Consequently, Roman Catholic institutions were founded by each of the major nationality groups: Irish, German, Italian, Polish, and Czech.

About 1890 Roman Catholics began to establish settlements and other group-work agencies for the assistance of new immigrants. Many hospitals and homes for the aged were also established about this time.

The various social welfare institutions of the Roman Catholic Church were related to its parishes, dioceses, or orders, but their work was not co-ordinated. Consequently, the National Conference of Catholic Charities was established in 1910, with its headquarters in Washington. It not only co-ordinated established welfare work, but also stimulated the formation of local conferences of Catholic charities, gave a place to the lay leaders of the church, and helped to bridge the gap between Roman Catholic welfare services and those of the rest of the country.

Protestantism. The closing of the monasteries of England disrupted a system of relief that had been in operation for many generations. Since the number of the poor was increasing, it was necessary to develop a new and more effective system for meeting their needs. The English kings decided that they could no longer rely on voluntary relief alone, but must levy compulsory taxes for this purpose. The "Poor Laws" enacted in the late sixteenth and early seventeenth centuries in England placed responsibility on each parish to levy taxes and provide for the needs of dependent children, the aged, and the unemployed. A minimum of relief was given in this way, and it was expected that the funds would be supplemented by voluntary benevolence.

The faith that the Pilgrims brought to America and that later became Congregationalism played a significant part in developing Protestant policies concerning social welfare. In seventeenth and eighteenth century New England, the church was very closely related to the town government. It was customary for the town to set aside land on the village green for a meeting house, to provide for its erection, and to give a stipend to the minister. In many cases, citizenship in the town was open only to members of the church. The citizens believed that they had a covenant with God to govern their personal and community affairs according to his will. They felt that they were bound by the laws of God whether they were voting in one of the business sessions of the church or in a town meeting. In this setting and following the example of the Poor Laws of England, the citizens voted to use town funds for the care of the needy and for the establishment of such institutions as were necessary. Thus, in early New England the basic needs of the poor were met by the town government; only supplemental help was given by the church.

In the United States of the eighteenth and nineteenth centuries, the same conditions that led Roman Catholics to establish agencies and institutions of social welfare led Protestants to do so, also. The increase in the number of persons who were unable to take care of themselves during this period was due to a combination of factors:

the industrial revolution, increased immigration, rapid growth of cities, and catastrophic epidemics. Some denominations tended to provide for needy members of their own congregations through agencies and institutions established and operated by the church. Others believed that private and government agencies should be established that would serve all persons regardless of their faith. These denominations encouraged their members to take part in the formation and supervision of such institutions, but established very few of their own.

One of the first child-care institutions established in the United States was the Bethesda Home for Boys, near Savannah, Georgia, which was founded in 1740 by a Methodist, George Whitefield, acting on the suggestion of Charles Wesley.

Many of the non-sectarian agencies for social welfare were started under the impetus of Protestants, both laymen and clergymen. There is room for only two examples: Robert M. Hartley, a devoutly religious English businessman, was the founder of The Association for Improving the Conditions of the Poor, organized in New York in 1842; a minister, Martin Van Buren Arsdale, was the originator of the Children's Home Society Movement of the late nineteenth century. Both agencies drew their support primarily from Protestants, but they served all persons in need, regardless of religion.

Laymen, with some assistance from the clergy, formed many interdenominational societies for the purpose of teaching the poor to read, supplying them with Bibles and tracts, and encouraging their interest in missionary work at home and abroad. Among the most successful of these organizations were the American Bible Society, American Home Missionary Society, American Sunday-School Union, and American Tract Society. They made great contributions toward the establishment of churches in the West and the inculcation of habits of thrift and virtue in the heterogeneous people of the United States. The interdenominational movement that made possible such operative organizations had started earlier in England, but reached its fullest development in the United States between 1816 and 1837.

The response that Protestants made to poverty was not always to improve the living conditions of the poor. One response was to congratulate them on their freedom from the temptations that accompany wealth and to assure them that a short life of poverty and pain on earth would be rewarded by eternal bliss in heaven.

Preaching in the late nineteenth and early twentieth centuries began to help Christians see that fullness of life was intended for all people and that old concepts of charity and individual concern were too small. If God is Lord of all life his ways must be followed not only in personal relations, but in social, economic, and political affairs, as well. Attention was turning from ameliorating the situation of the poor and needy to establishing social justice. Jane Addams expressed this position in an address in 1910:

Religious Origins of Social Work

It would be easy . . . to trace the gradual steps by which charitable folk were irresistibly led from Cure to Prevention, as it would also be possible to demonstrate . . . that we are now being led in the same gradual but unresting manner from Prevention to a consideration of Vital Welfare. The negative policy of relieving destitution, or even the more generous one of preventing it, is giving way to the positive idea of raising life to its highest value.[1]

Early in the twentieth century the churches began to establish national commissions for social education and action. These denominational agencies have a dual function: to educate church members about social, economic, and political problems; and to assist them in taking effective social action. They co-operate with one another and with the Division of Christian Life and Work of the National Council of Churches. They have made substantial contributions to numerous changes in national social policy, and are becoming an increasingly potent force for social justice in the most complex and important areas of human concern in our society.

Protestant churches operate many social agencies and institutions. The denominational boards responsible for this part of the work of the churches co-operate with the Department of Social Welfare of the National Council of Churches. Together they are playing an ever increasing role in raising the standards of social welfare work in the United States.

[1] Johnson, Emily Cooper, ed. *Jane Addams: A Centennial Reader,* p. 85. New York: The Macmillan Co., 1960. Used by permission.

RESPONSIBILITY OF THE CHURCHES
FOR SOCIAL WELFARE

Throughout much of human history the home and the church have carried the major responsibility for social welfare. We have mentioned the beginning of governmental sharing in this responsibility in England with the passage of the Poor Laws, and the provisions for the poor made by town governments in early New England. But it is only within the last half century that agencies of the Federal Government of the United States have given greater assistance to more persons than have the churches. This increased participation by government must not cause us to forget that the concept of social service grew out of religious faith and must continue to be nourished by its roots. If the needs of persons who cannot take care of themselves are to be met with intelligence, generosity, and grace, churches and other religious bodies must continue to take an active part in the whole field of social welfare. Our responsibility does not end with the maintenance of a few agencies and institutions, but includes Christian concern about the work done by private and government agencies.

CHAPTER THREE

Children and Youth

Let the children come to me, and do not hinder them;
for to such belongs the kingdom of heaven. —Matthew
19:14.

A nation's most valuable resource is its children and
youth. Its future depends upon their vitality, training, and
vision. The United States is blessed with more than 65
million persons nineteen years of age or younger. The
number of children and young people living in the country
today exceeds the total population of 1890.

Even though the number of children and young people
is increasing at a rapid rate, their proportion in the total
population is decreasing. In 1850, children and youth nineteen years of age and younger made up 52.5 per cent of the
population; in 1958 their proportion of the whole was only
37.9. During those same years the proportion of persons in
the prime of life, 20 to 64, increased from 44.9 to 53.5 per
cent. This means that the adults should be able to make
ample provision for all children and for other persons who
are unable to provide for themselves.

Every child has the right to grow up in a home where he

is wanted and loved by a father and mother who provide for his physical, cultural, educational, and spiritual needs. Many of the 65 million children and young people in the United States have the good fortune to live in such homes, but two or three million others do not. Christians care deeply about the welfare of all children, but they are particularly concerned about those who are neglected and handicapped.

ORPHANAGES ESTABLISHED IN THE LATE NINETEENTH CENTURY

In Colonial America and in the early days of the republic, the needs of orphans and other dependent children were met by their relatives or by the local church. If a child was left alone, members of the Ladies' Aid Society would find a suitable family that was willing to adopt him or give him a foster home. Although the first Protestant home for children in America was founded in 1740, it was not until after the Civil War that many such homes were necessary. Numerous children were made homeless by that fratricidal carnage and thousands more were orphaned by the epidemics that followed the mass migration of Europeans to America in the late nineteenth century. Since local churches could not provide homes for so many children, district, state, and national bodies of the churches established institutional homes for them. Those homes were designed to serve children of particular denominations, and the inculcation of the faith was a dominant element.

CHANGING NEEDS

There are far fewer orphans in proportion to the population today than there were in the nineteenth century. Better living conditions and improved health facilities have prolonged the lives of parents. Only 3 per cent of the children who need benevolent help today are full orphans.

Not only are there fewer orphans; the convictions about how they should be reared have changed. Christians believe that the family has been instituted by God and that children ought to be reared within a family group. Practically all workers with children agree that orphans should live with families, rather than in institutions. They try to place homeless children for adoption and to provide foster homes for those who are not adopted.

Among the children and young people today who have special needs that cannot be met by their families are:

Children who need financial assistance because their families are unable to provide the necessities of life for them

Orphans and other children who need temporary care in an institution and placement in an adoptive or foster home

Children who are handicapped by emotional maladjustment, mental retardation, blindness, partial loss of vision, deafness, impaired hearing, crippled limbs, speech defects, and other physical handicaps

Children who are delinquent or pre-delinquent

How are the needs of these children being met? What are the churches doing to help? Let us consider each group in turn.

CHILDREN WHO NEED FINANCIAL ASSISTANCE

By far the largest number of children who need help are those who live with one or both parents, but in homes where the family incomes are too low to provide adequately for them. The parents may be unemployed or they may be among the nearly 20 per cent of American families who live in poverty.

THE AID TO DEPENDENT CHILDREN program is a cooperative venture of Federal, state, and local governments. In August, 1959, 2,911,000 children were aided by this program. The average monthly payment per child was $28.33.

While some churches give small allowances to a few families for the care of children for brief periods, churches as a whole do very little to aid those children whose primary need is for material assistance. This need is met almost entirely by government agencies.

NORMAL CHILDREN IN NEED OF HOMES

Protestant churches carry a large share of the responsibility for providing homes for neglected children. Who are these children? Many of them are infants born out of wedlock. Others come from homes which have disintegrated because of death, desertion, separation of the parents, or a combination of these factors.

Finding homes for homeless children.   Church agencies

do everything in their power to find adoptive homes for all children who need them. More than thirty agencies for the placement and adoption of children are related to Protestant denominations. A brief review of the work of one such agency will indicate the type of service these agencies render.

THE ADOPTION SERVICE OF THE LUTHERAN WELFARE SOCIETY OF IOWA employs a trained staff that seeks to find the right home for the right child. It holds group meetings to inform couples about the responsibilities of and procedures for becoming adoptive parents. The prospective parents and the child are carefully examined and their suitability for each other is determined.

Each year, approximately seven hundred thousand couples in the United States seek to adopt children. At present there are not this many children available annually for adoption, but the gap is narrowing steadily between prospective homes and the number of children who need them.

Care in foster homes. It may be necessary to place children in foster homes until the conditions in their own homes are suitable for their return; or they may need to live in them for an indefinite period. Children who are placed in foster homes by a church agency receive much the same kind of care as children in any good home. The foster parents are selected and supervised by the child-placing agency; a social caseworker visits the home regularly; and consultation service is available when it is needed.

One example of the type of agency that renders this service is the Inter-church Child Care Society of Pennsylvania, a Protestant agency in Philadelphia. In 1959 it maintained 226 boys and girls in foster homes and placed six for adoption.

While there are more prospective parents than there are children available for permanent adoption, there is a dearth of foster homes. Some churches are helping to remedy this situation through a program of information. For example, The Federation of Protestant Welfare Agencies in New York City conducts a Foster Home Finding Service that has procured hundreds of homes for use by the child-placing agencies affiliated with it.

Care for children in institutions. Although far fewer normal children need the services of a home than did a generation ago, some still require this type of care. Many of the residents of church homes stay in them for one or two years and then return to their own homes or go to live with relatives. Many teenagers find it easier to adapt to life in institutions than in foster homes. Some children must live in institutions because they have problems that are too difficult for a private family to handle.

THE PRESBYTERIAN HOME FOR CHILDREN, Farmington, Missouri, is representative of church homes for normal children. One hundred boys and girls from five to eighteen years of age lead happy, busy lives there. The children attend the public school and participate in the life of local churches. Each child is given the constructive experience of contributing some labor to the running of the home. Thirty-six teen-age boys live on a dairy and chicken farm at the edge of town, where they share in the work of the farm and learn modern agricultural methods.

Many church homes have discontinued services to normal children and now devote their resources to the highly specialized care of one or more types of handicapped children. They work with children who are emotionally disturbed, mentally retarded, or physically handicapped. Most of the homes that render these highly specialized services were formerly orphanages that cared for normal children. When the number of children who needed this type of institutional care dwindled, the homes studied the needs of their areas. The choice of the new field of work was frequently made in consultation with state departments of public welfare and the Child Welfare League of America, Inc.

EMOTIONALLY DISTURBED CHILDREN

When a child is subjected to too many pressures, he may become so disturbed emotionally that he must be separated from his former environment in order to be restored to health. If such a child has the good fortune to live in a church home for disturbed children for two or three years he may be able to resume life in the community. Two stories illustrate the types of problems these children face:

Jean was the youngest of six children, all of whom were older and lived away from home. Jean's mother was separated from her father and worked to support the family. When Jean was eleven she was expelled from school because of extreme temper tantrums and frequent epileptic seizures. When the director of a church home called to get her, she was where she had been for days—sitting in an old chair, clutching a toy panda bear. Jean was very unattractive, but she longed for attention from her mother. The only way she knew to get it was to throw a temper tantrum.

Henry was the bashful, backward, unattractive son of a successful professional man. His older sister was bright, alert, and brilliant in school. Their mother contrasted Henry unfavorably with his sister and urged him to equal her achievements. He wanted to please his mother, but he could not attain the success of his more capable sister. His failure to do so worried him so much that he was on the verge of a mental breakdown when he was admitted to a home for disturbed children.

Churches provide homes for disturbed children. An increasing number of church agencies are working with disturbed children. The American Baptist Home Mission Societies report that the majority of their fourteen homes for children are working with disturbed rather than with normal children. Brief accounts of the programs of several denominational homes will indicate the type of work that is being done:

ALEXANDER HOME, in Charlotte, North Carolina, is owned by the Presbyterian, U.S., churches of Mecklenburg County. It was operated as an orphanage from its founding in 1903 to 1947. It now conducts a highly specialized treatment program for boys and girls between the ages of six and twelve who are severely disturbed emotionally but normal otherwise. Children live in four groups of not more than seven each. The staff consists of the director, five resident counselors, two recreation workers, one remedial teacher, one medical worker, one caseworker, one housekeeper-dietician, and seven office and maintenance workers. About half the children are able to attend the public schools; the others receive remedial instruction at the home. The professionally trained caseworker not only works with the children, but also gives therapeutic and interpretative help to their parents.

SPOFFORD HOME, Kansas City, Missouri, took care of dependent but normal children from its founding in 1916 to 1940. It is affiliated with the Woman's Division of Christian Service of The Methodist Church. Since 1940, the home has cared for emotionally disturbed boys and girls between six and twelve. Children who enter Spofford are unhappy and at war with the world. After two or three years of psychiatric guidance and loving care, most of them have been helped to the extent that they are able to resume normal life in the community.

THE LUTHERAN CHILDREN'S HOME SOCIETY, Waverly, Iowa, is affiliated with The American Lutheran Church. It was founded during the Civil War to serve orphaned and dependent children, but during the late 1940's and 1950's gradually developed its program to provide psychotherapy for children having emotional disturbances (including character disorders). The home serves children primarily from the state of Iowa, but also accepts referrals from other states.

In addition to three groups of children in the open institutional setting, two groups are served in a closed setting where they receive highly individualized care to promote an optimum feeling of security and the sense of being completely cared for. These latter facilities are called Hospital Units and plans are already completed for the erection of a new Hospital-Admissions Center. The home also operates two group foster homes in the community (but not on campus) for children who have derived maximum benefit from institutional care, but are not yet ready for private family life, or who have arrived at a semi-independent status. The home provides outpatient service to parents of children in residence and to children and parents in the Waverly community.

The staff consists of an executive director, medical director who is also the consulting psychiatrist, psychologist, eight to ten trained caseworkers, twenty to twenty-four group care and recreation workers, three full-time teachers in the Campus School, two full-time tutors, several part-time tutors, four office secretaries, four kitchen workers, ten to twelve maintenance and housekeeping workers. About three fourths of the children attend Campus School and/or are in private tutoring situations, since some are too ill to benefit from instruction even in small groups.

The Lutheran Children's Home Society is accredited by the Child Welfare League of America.

CHILDREN WHO ARE MENTALLY RETARDED

Americans are beginning to understand the problem of persons who are mentally retarded, and churches are beginning to take their share of responsibility for helping such individuals.

It is estimated that thirty out of every thousand babies are born with mental deficiencies. This means that about 3 per cent of the population of the United States may be mentally retarded. The Intelligence Quotients (IQ) for normal persons range from 90 to 110; those with IQ's of 75 to 90 are called "slow learners." Persons whose IQ's fall below 75 are considered mentally retarded.

Causes of mental retardation.   Research is yielding information about the causes of mental retardation. A retarded child can be born to any parents. There are at least ninety conditions, injuries, and diseases that may cause retardation, most of which occur before or during birth. Among the causes are glandular disturbance in the mother, German measles during pregnancy, and a long or difficult childbirth. In some cases, retardation is due to hereditary causes.

Twenty-five out of thirty mentally retarded persons have IQ's ranging from 50 to 75; they are educable, but need especially designed courses of study. Most of these people will become self-supporting and socially independent. Four of the thirty are trainable, with IQ's ranging from 25 to 50.

They can learn to care for their own personal needs, to work under close supervision, and to earn their own living under sheltered conditions. One out of every thirty retarded persons (or one out of every thousand persons in the population) is so retarded that his mind will not develop beyond that of a baby.

The child welfare agencies of several demominations have done pioneering work with mentally retarded children. Let us look briefly at their work and then consider the responsibility of local churches for mentally retarded persons and their families.

Churches maintain homes and schools. Several denominations support homes and agencies designed to give mentally retarded children the training that will enable them to use all the ability they have. A brief review of the work of a school and a home will provide some understanding of this kind of effort.

EVERGREEN PRESBYTERIAN VOCATION SCHOOL, Minden, Louisiana, is a new venture of the Presbyterian Church, U.S. Established in 1959, it is a residential school for mentally retarded youths from sixteen to twenty-six years of age. The school offers a four-year course of vocational training in agriculture or industrial arts. There are also classes in art, ceramics, and music. There is a counseling program for students and their parents. Some students will go directly from the school to employment; others will require an additional year of training on the job before employment.

MARTIN LUTHER HOME, Beatrice, Nebraska, is a residential home for boys and girls that is related to the American Lutheran Church. There are four basic class programs, which help prepare mentally retarded children for a self-reliant life. The school has room for seventy residential and fifteen day students, but there are always students on the waiting list.

Three other Lutheran agencies for the training of mentally retarded children are the Vasa Lutheran Home for Children, Red Wing, Minnesota; Lutheran Children's Home, Fergus Falls, Minnesota; and the West River Crippled Children's Hospital and School, Hot Springs, South Dakota, which trains children who are not only mentally retarded but crippled as well.

The Protestant Episcopal Church provides two day schools for mentally retarded children: The Sheltering Arms in Minneapolis, Minnesota, and The St. John's Development Service for Children in Washington, D.C. The Disciples of Christ are building a home at Columbia, Missouri, which will serve persons who are mentally deficient and/or physically defective.   **1192099**

Local churches begin to accept responsibility for mentally retarded children. About 5 per cent of the Americans who are mentally retarded live in institutions, but the remaining 95 per cent live at home. This means that local churches can be of great help to them and their families. There are at least four ways in which they can be of service:

GIVE HELP TO THE FAMILIES. The realization that the new baby does not have normal intelligence can be a great shock to a family. The minister and members of the church can help the family weather this crisis and find the spiritual grace to accept the child and give him the training that he needs for a useful, satisfying life.

INFORM THE CONGREGATION ABOUT MENTAL RETARDATION. One of the greatest contributions that churches can make is to understand the causes of mental retardation and to make them known in the church and community. They should also help people understand that proper training will enable children to live happily within their limitations.

OFFER CHRISTIAN EDUCATION AND CHURCH MEMBERSHIP TO RETARDED PERSONS. Persons who are retarded have as great need for the Christian gospel as do others. They should be welcomed into church membership, and a program of Christian education should be developed to meet their needs. Children who are not seriously retarded may make more progress when placed in classes with boys and girls of their own age groups. Since children who are seriously retarded require special classes, it may be necessary for several churches to co-operate in developing a good program of Christian education for them. Councils of churches have taken the lead in organizing such programs in some cities. The Belfield Avenue Church (Evangelical United Brethren) is host to such a co-operative effort in Philadelphia. Only fifty-five such programs are in operation in the Protestant churches of the United States.

DEVELOP PROGRAMS OF CHRISTIAN EDUCATION IN HOMES.
If no program of Christian education exists in a home for
the mentally retarded, local churches can help to provide
one.

CHILDREN WHO ARE PHYSICALLY HANDICAPPED

The church is deeply concerned about the children who
must go through life with physical handicaps: the crippled,
the blind, those with limited vision, the deaf, those with impaired hearing, and those with more than one handicap.
In the recent past, there was little that could be done for
the handicapped except to give them custodial care, but
miracles are now being performed that enable the lame to
walk, the blind to see, and the deaf to hear. Just as great
miracles are being performed to help those whose abilities
cannot be restored; they are learning to use hands and ears
in place of eyes, toes in place of fingers, arms in place of
legs. The learning process is usually a long and costly one.
It requires the utmost courage, exertion, and patience on
the part of the handicapped child and highly skilled and
compassionate service from physicians, nurses, teachers,
and caretakers. In spite of all these difficulties, thousands
of young people "graduate" from homes and hospitals
every year, equipped to earn their living, to establish families,
and to take part in church and community life.

What are churches doing to help handicapped children?

They are helping in four major ways: by providing therapy and training for a few children; by providing chaplaincy service at state institutions; by including handicapped persons in the life of the congregation; and by rendering volunteer service in homes and hospitals.

Churches provide therapy and training. Most of the institutions that provide therapy, education, and rehabilitation for physically handicapped children are operated by private or government agencies; however, a few such homes are maintained by several denominations. Two examples follow:

THE CRIPPLED CHILDREN'S SCHOOL, Jamestown, North Dakota, is doing notable work. It is owned and operated by the Lutheran Hospitals and Homes Society of America, Inc. It accepts children with severe physical disabilities who have fairly normal mental ability. It offers an educational program from kindergarten through high school and a two-year business course. A therapy rehabilitation program is co-ordinated with scholastic training. Children who need it are given physical, occupational, and speech therapy. A pre-vocational evaluation unit helps each child discover the work that he can do with most ease and satisfaction. Girls are helped to learn the art of homemaking within the limits of their handicaps. The school can serve about eighty students at a time. Its income is from tuition and donations.

THE HOUSE OF ST. GILES THE CRIPPLE, affiliated with the Episcopal Diocese of Long Island, has conducted a program of operative and therapeutic treatment of physically handicapped children for more than fifty years. Recently, it has shifted its emphasis from the care of victims of poliomyelitis to children with cerebral palsy.

Churches provide chaplaincy service at state and private institutions. Many Protestant ministers serve as full or part-time chaplains at homes and hospitals for the disabled. The Ephphatha Missions of the American Lutheran Church maintains a pastor in Faribault, Minnesota, who works with the children in the state schools for the deaf and blind which are located there; it also maintains a pastor at the South Dakota State School for the Deaf in Sioux Falls.

Churches provide for the handicapped in their programs. Many churches make it easier for handicapped persons to participate in the life of the congregation in such ways as by arranging transportation for them, by installing loud speakers, by building ramps that will accommodate wheel chairs. The experience of one local church with the deaf is illustrative of what churches can do to include handicapped persons in their regular programs:

THE METHODIST CHURCH, Sioux Falls, South Dakota, sends a bus to the State School for the Deaf to bring the children to the church. The children from grades one through six participate in the regular classes, while those in junior and senior high have special classes taught by teachers from the School for the Deaf. The deaconess, Miss Judith Dunnell, taught a membership class of eleven deaf children, who together with fifty-two hearing youth, joined the church on Mother's Day. She writes of her experience in teaching the class:

For three months we had worked on one lesson in the church membership manual. . . . For three long months we had explored together the meaning of Holy Communion. . . . What a thrill it was for me to be kneeling with them as they took the bread and juice to the "comfort of their souls" and, as they rose from the table, to see the brightness in their eyes! This was a new experience of Jesus and a new understanding of forgiveness for them. . . . There are times when . . . teaching these children is very frustrating because of lack of communication, but then, during such moments as the Communion Service I feel it is worth all the effort. . . . I am hoping that some day we will be able to serve these persons as well as we serve the hearing persons.[1]

Church members render volunteer service. Many church members render invaluable service on a voluntary basis in church homes and in those operated by the state and other agencies. The forms of service vary widely. The church may ask its members to visit the home regularly; the young people may plan parties for the children; the young adult class of the church may prepare programs for presentation at the home; the women's society may take food and clothing to the home. One example of such service is rendered by college students:

THE TARTAN TROUPERS OF MACALESTER COLLEGE

[1] "Hear Him, Ye Deaf!" by Judith Dunnell, in *The Methodist Woman,* September, 1960, pp. 15-16. Used by permission.

(United Presbyterian), St. Paul, Minnesota, is a project of the Westminster Fellowship. The troupe is made up of sixty student magicians, singers, comedians, bagpipers, and other entertainers. Usually they take their show to hospitals, orphanages, and schools, where they are enthusiastically received by the children. Each spring the troupers hold a Children's Carnival in the college gym. Five-hundred orphaned and handicapped children come to the carnival, escorted by student hosts.

PREVENTING JUVENILE DELINQUENCY

The term "juvenile delinquency" is widely used in America today, but its meaning varies greatly. Sometimes it refers merely to defiance or ungovernability on the part of young people. A more precise meaning of the term is: the commission of misdemeanors (minor crimes) or felonies (major crimes) by children and youths. Obviously, only juvenile offenders apprehended by the penal authorities can be authoritatively classified as delinquents in this sense and many crimes go undetected.

Since there is no uniformity in the way courts classify "juveniles" or in the popularly used definitions of "delinquency," there can be no accurate assessment of the extent of juvenile delinquency. However, it is known that more than 1,700,000 children in the United States have records of delinquency—have been arrested, brought before a court, and convicted of crimes. The Federal Bureau of Investigation reports that more than half of all major crimes are committed by persons under twenty-one years of age. Authorities agree that the rate of juvenile delinquency is increasing more rapidly than the population. Despite these facts, it is estimated that not more than 3 per cent of America's children and youth are juvenile delinquents. It is also true that many youthful offenders grow into law-abiding adults.

What causes juvenile delinquency?   There are many causes of juvenile delinquency, but there is no general agreement as to what they are. Among the factors that are thought to contribute to it are "delinquent" parents, loneliness, poverty, broken homes, working mothers, fathers who lack authority, weak discipline in home and school, inadequate rehabilitation of first offenders, vicious comic books, inadequate programs of work and recreation for children and youth. When these environmental factors are given as causes of juvenile delinquency, the question remains unanswered as to why some children subjected to these conditions become delinquents, while others do not. Slums breed delinquency, yet millions of sturdy citizens spent their early years in the slums. Rejection or overindulgence of children by parents have contributed to the growing list of offenders, but many youngsters who suffered the impact of these same experiences did not become delinquents. Children and youth from "rich" homes as well as from "poor," from "right" neighborhoods as well as from "wrong" have gotten into trouble.

The program of the local church.   What are the churches

doing to prevent juvenile delinquency? Their work ranges from their own programs of Christian education, through general programs designed to keep youngsters out of mischief, to work with young people who have been convicted of crimes. Brief summaries of several types of work follow:

Several million children and young people participate in the programs of Christian education in thousands of Protestant churches. This experience helps most of the participants to develop into constructive Christian citizens. Many programs of Christian education, however, are far less effective than they should be in reaching the young people who are aggressive, confused, and disturbed.

FIRST PRESBYTERIAN CHURCH, Avenel, New Jersey, had the foresight to change its policy regarding young people. It had six members in its Sunday evening fellowship, but the church was surrounded by teen-agers who were falling into delinquency. There were thefts, narcotics addiction, beatings; hanging around the street corners were crowds that might easily become full-fledged, organized gangs. The town's population had trebled in a decade, and the old residents resented the newcomers. The church decided that it would use its resources to serve the young people. The church parlor that had been reserved for adults was converted into a basketball court and skating rink. The minister and the young people of the church launched "operation streetscraping"—they roamed the streets and told the youths they met of the new program at the church. After a year, the Sunday evening group had grown to forty, but scores of teen-agers come to the church on week nights to take part in sports, learn hobbies, and dance. At first the program was largely recreational, but later a religious dimension was added. Soon it was necessary to erect a new building for the youth center. Now six hundred young people take part in its activities, two hundred attend church school, and one out of every five persons in the worship services is a teen-ager. Potential delinquents have become faithful Christians.

THE JUVENILE PROTECTION PROGRAM of the American Baptist Home Mission Societies is a program through which leaders at the national level help local churches plan week-day activities that are geared particularly to the needs of young people in their own communities. To initiate a local program, a survey of the needs and problems of the youth of the community is made, plus a study of the facilities and leadership of the church. With these two factors in mind, the leaders of the church plan those programs that seem most suitable. Some of the techniques that have been used to reach troubled children and youth are: boys' and girls' clubs, which may be special interest or friendship groups; recreation, such as parties, youth canteens, camping, hiking, drama, craft, hobbies, and athletics; family living institutes, in which counseling is given; and foster home care.

Settlements and Christian centers. Many Protestant churches have established settlements or Christian centers in congested areas of American cities. The American Baptist Home Mission Societies maintain forty such centers

44

throughout the United States. While these centers serve all age groups, they have been particularly successful with teen-agers. A report indicates the success of the program:

Miraculously, a Christian center can reach the friendless youths in the thirteen to twenty year old group who have knocked around the streets and the saloons, stolen a few cars for joy rides, burglarized a gas station, been involved in a shoot-ing or knifing, and spent some time in a reform school. . . . A guy can join a basketball game in the gym and still not burn the bridges of gang respect behind him.

Interfaith Neighbors.   Interfaith Neighbors is the name a group of churches and synagogues have given their co-operative program for the prevention of juvenile delin-quency on the Upper East Side of New York. The organiza-tion employs workers who deal with young people on their own territory—the street. The workers are usually on the street five nights a week. They may be up all night helping a boy to deal with a drunken father or talking with a nar-cotics addict about his problems. The street workers help to get jobs for boys who need them. They are alert to the prob-lems of boys who have returned from reform school. This approach has been so successful with boys that Interfaith Neighbors now employs a woman to work with girls.

The street workers keep close contact with the youth pa-trolmen of the area. Since its organization Interfaith Neigh-bors has twice been asked by the police authorities to expand its work. This has been accomplished through added sup-port from the churches and synagogues, and the work is still growing. A committee of volunteer laymen from the member groups supplement the professional workers in appropriate cases.

Group work with youth in conflict. For fifty years the ATLANTIC STREET CENTER in Seattle, Washington, an agency related to The Methodist Church, carried on a varied program that included work with the aged, summer day camps, youth work, urban renewal, and a special project with socially maladjusted youth. In 1959, the center decided to concentrate all of its resources on work with socially maladjusted youth and to transfer its other programs to related agencies.

The center now works with boys of junior high age who are known to the police or to the Juvenile Court. It accepts individuals and gangs of boys, but works with them in clubs of nine persons or less. The experience of Fred illustrates how the center assists youths who are on the verge of delinquency:

Fred is the second of seven children. His father served a term in the penitentiary for the use of narcotics; he drifts in and out of his home. Fred's mother has been arrested for fighting, prostitution, and maltreatment of the children. Because of injurious living conditions, the children were placed in foster homes for two years, but eventually they were returned to their mother. In the spring of 1960, Fred was expelled because of repeated misbehavior in school. He was referred to the court because of assault and thefts, but was released on probation at the recommendation of a worker from the center. Fred entered into the life of the center, but asked to be transferred from one club to another with more internal cohesion. He entered summer school and finished his work with no problems of behavior. He re-entered junior high and is gradually changing his values. He has begun to get a sense of self-worth and to have some appreciation for others. Fred found in the worker at the center a person who disapproved of his delinquent behavior but accepted and cared for him as a human being. This was a new and vital experience for Fred, who said to the worker during a camping trip: "I've waited a long time to be happy, but now I am."

Counsel for juvenile delinquents and pre-delinquents. Two examples will illustrate the type of counsel that churches offer to delinquents and pre-delinquents:

THE EPISCOPAL CITY MISSION SOCIETY OF MISSOURI gives pastoral care to Protestant children who are brought before the Juvenile Court. A Youth Consultation Service has been developed that serves young people before they reach the crisis of a court experience.

CHAPLAINCY SERVICE. When a Protestant child is sent to the Philadelphia Youth Study Center to await sentence by the Juvenile Court, one of the first persons he meets is Tom C. Cooke, a chaplain supported by the United Presbyterian Church in the U.S.A. Even though most children remain in the center only a few weeks or months, they soon come to know Tom Cooke as a friend. Any child may ask for an interview with him, and many of them do. Or they may participate in one of his group counseling sessions or take part in the program of Christian education, which is staffed with volunteers from Philadelphia churches. Mr.

Cooke reports that he gets to know children better in two weeks at the center than he did in two years in his former parish. He says:

We try to help children . . . learn that although they must see through the almost natural consequences of their behavior, the process . . . can be an experience of growth. Our purpose is not that these children should come through this experience unscarred, for that is impossible, but rather that the scar they bear may serve to remind them of the love of God which heals wounds, and of the people of God who stand ready to help them, with a concern motivated by the love of God.[1]

EVALUATION OF PROTESTANT WORK
WITH CHILDREN AND YOUTH

The number of church-related agencies and institutions that serve children is impressive. In 1955, the National Council of Churches conducted a survey of the welfare agencies related to Protestant churches. Fifty denominations replied; thirty-seven said that they operated agencies and institutions in the field of social welfare; fourteen reported that they did not. The thirty-seven denominations indicated that they maintained 126 homes for children, 30 agencies for child placement and adoption, 22 day nurseries and 25 other agencies whose primary purpose was to serve children. In addition to maintaining these 202 agencies, they reported that work with children was one of the purposes of 494 other church-related agencies. This means that thirty-seven

[1] "Because He First Loved Us," by Tom C. Cooke, in *Presbyterian Life*, August 1, 1959, p. 36. Used by permission.

Protestant denominations maintain 696 agencies whose purposes includes service to children.

Is the church pioneering in child welfare today? When the churches established orphanages in the late nineteenth century they were taking an adventurous step to meet a new situation. A number of homes for children have discontinued general work with normal children and devote their resources to specialized work with children who are handicapped physically, mentally, or socially.

It is possible that many other homes and agencies should look critically at the work they are doing. Could the needs of the normal children now in their care be met more adequately in the children's own homes or in adoptive or foster homes? Are there exceptional children in the area whose needs the church should be meeting? Are the emotions of board and staff members so deeply involved in the work the agency is now doing that they cannot consider the possibility of others doing it?

The work that a very few churches and church agencies are doing to prevent juvenile delinquency indicates how much more needs to be done. Have we found the most creative way for the church to help children who are in conflict with society? Does the group-work approach of the Atlantic Street Center offer the best method? Or is the street-worker approach of Interfaith Neighbors more effective? Or is Archie Hargraves, pastor of the Nazarene Congregational Church in Brooklyn, right when he says that tough city youngsters are much more interested in the essential contribution that the church can make to their lives than they are in its recreational programs? He says that they long for the sense of direction found in the Christian faith, for the acceptance and love of God found in the Christian church. Do we offer young people the fruits of our faith, rather than help them find their own faith?

How high are the standards of work? Some of the best work in the field of social welfare—and some of the poorest—is being done by church-related agencies. One indication that many church-related homes and other agencies are doing work of poor caliber is the fact that only a few of them meet the membership requirements of the Child Welfare League of America, Inc., the national standard-setting agency in the field.

Another indication of the poor quality of work done in some church agencies and institutions is found in the nature of the recommendations one national church body thought it necessary to make to its child welfare agencies. It exhorts them "to conform to or exceed the health and safety laws . . . regardless of any exemptions which may be made for homes operated under church auspices." While most states require church agencies to conform to their requirements for health and safety, some do not. But should any church-related agency take advantage of such leniency and fail to meet these standards?

Who bears the cost? The publicity folders of many church-related agencies and institutions indicate that church bodies supply only a small fraction of the cost of

their operations. The survey made by the National Council
of Churches in 1955, mentioned earlier, indicated the total
income and its sources for two types of children's agencies.
The 126 institutions for the care of children had receipts
that totaled $11,887,000. The thirty agencies for child
placement and adoption reported that their total income
was $3,647,000. The percentage figures for the sources of
this income are as follows:

Sources of Income	*In-stitutional Care*	*Child Placement and Adoption*
Service fees, investments, etc.	37.7	45.7
Contributions from church organizations	38.7	31.0
Contributions from individuals	11.9	7.7
Contributions from Community Chests	4.0	9.0
Contributions from public funds	2.3	1.1
All other types of contributed income	5.4	5.5

It is significant that church organizations contributed
about one third of the money needed to operate these agencies—more than a third of the cost for institutional care and
slightly less than a third in the case of child placement
and adoption.

*What should be the contribution of the church to work
with children?* Should Christians feel guilty because
church agencies carry such a small part of the total burden
of providing for children with special needs? Should

churches raise tremendous sums of money in order to develop more agencies and institutions to serve children?

Perhaps the church should maintain only a limited number of agencies and institutions. Rather than trying to equip and maintain homes, hospitals, and other agencies to meet all types of situations, perhaps the church should encourage private and government agencies to carry these responsibilities to the greatest possible degree. Then the church would be free to render more distinctly Christian services in these homes and agencies. Perhaps the maintenance of a chaplaincy service at every state-supported home and agency for children would be of more significance than spending the same amount of money in building new church-related agencies.

Sometimes an agency renders a greater service by co-operating with another organization to see that a need is met than by stretching its own resources to meet it. The experience of one church-related center illustrates this fact:

BETHLEHEM CENTER, Fort Worth, Texas, a Methodist agency, was asked to add a class for retarded children to its overcrowded program. The board and staff studied the problem and then conferred with a similar agency. It seemed clear to all that this project should be undertaken but that it should be done by a third agency: The Tarrant County Association for Mental Health. Bethlehem Center continued to co-operate in development of the project: by finding room for the class in a public school; by helping to secure support from the United Community Fund; and by assisting the Association for Mental Health to get equipment and locate the children who needed the class.

If you would have something well done, you need not necessarily do it yourself; perhaps you should find the right persons to do it. In some cases, new facilities for children need to be provided by the churches; in others they should be developed by community agencies, public or private. Perhaps churches should call upon their social action committees to survey the need, develop public opinion in support of the project, and encourage their members to work as Christian citizens to see that the facility is provided. After it is in operation, Christians should maintain an active interest in it to see that it fulfills the purpose for which it was intended and should offer themselves for voluntary service where this is needed.

CHAPTER FOUR

The Aging

> To be seventy years young is sometimes more cheerful
> and hopeful than to be forty years old. —Oliver Wen-
> dell Holmes

One of the phenomena of the twentieth century is the
great increase in the length of human life. Far more persons
can expect to live to be sixty, seventy, eighty, and even one
hundred than could have had such expectations in 1900. In
that year the life expectancy at birth was fifty years; in 1960
it was seventy.

The great gain in the average length of life is largely due
to the conquest of the contagious diseases of childhood and
youth. Comparatively little has been done to conquer the
diseases of age, but what has been done leads scientists to
wonder about the natural span of life for human beings.
Some researchers in this field believe that within the forsee-
able future, the *average* length of life will be one hundred
years!

When is a person old enough to be classed among the
aging? There can be no hard and fast answer to this question, since individuals age at different rates of speed. A man

of eighty may be younger, both physically and mentally, than a man of fifty. However, it is commonly agreed in both the United States and Canada that those who are sixty-five and over are among the aging, since that is the age when one becomes eligible for benefits under the Social Security System and under many private retirement plans.

GREAT INCREASE IN THE NUMBER OF AGING PERSONS

There are far more persons who are sixty-five and over in the United States and Canada than there have ever been before. They numbered more than 17 million in the United States in 1960; and 1,768,000 in Canada in 1956.

The aging constitute an ever-increasing proportion of the population. In 1900, persons sixty-five and over constituted 4.1 per cent of the population of the United States; but in 1958 their proportion had more than doubled to 8.6 per cent. Population experts expect that the proportion of older adults in the population will continue to increase and that by 1980 they will comprise 10 per cent of the population in Canada and 15 per cent in the United States.

THE ADDED YEARS CAN BE FULL OF LIFE

If the additional twenty years that the average person can expect to live merely prolonged the period of enfeeblement at the end of life, they would not be a boon but an intolerable burden. Many of these years, however, seem to be inserted just after the peak of man's productivity; they are years of somewhat less vigor than the preceding ones, but they are full of life and vitality. The years of enfeeblement may be somewhat longer also.

Most older people will lead productive lives for considerably more years than their grandparents did. Perhaps many of them will do their most productive work during these added years. They may emulate some of the great old men of the past: Sophocles, who wrote *Oedipus Rex* at seventy-five and organized the defense of Athens at eighty-three; Titian, who completed his great painting "The Battle of Lepanto" at ninety-five, Goethe, who completed *Faust* at eighty-three; Verdi, who composed the opera *Othello* at seventy-three and wrote the score for a *Te Deum* at eighty-five.

Despite the longer period of vitality that many older people are enjoying, some of them face very difficult problems. Let us consider some of these problems and see how churches are helping to meet them.

PROBLEMS OF AGING PERSONS

Some of the difficulties with which aging persons must cope are inevitable in the mysterious cycle of birth, life, and death; others are due to gross social injustice and can be corrected; some can be ameliorated by the thoughtfulness of the members of the Christian community.

Among the most acute problems that older adults face are these:

The Aging

Age restrictions on employment. If a person of forty or more is not already well established in his field, he has great difficulty in getting a job. Preference is given to younger workers, regardless of ability to do the job. Many employing groups have plans for compulsory retirement at the ages of sixty, sixty-five, or seventy; among these are commercial and industrial firms, government services, the armed forces, religious organizations, social agencies, and schools.

Inadequate incomes. Acute poverty is one of the gravest problems of elderly persons. More than 50 per cent of them subsist on per capita money incomes from all sources of less than $1,200 per year; and 80 per cent on less than $2,400. This is meager living indeed in the 1960's!

Lack of purpose for life. Work is such an important factor in North American culture that numerous persons seek employment who do not need to do so for economic reasons. One's work tends to define his status in society. Retirement under such circumstances can deal a serious blow to a person's ego. Not only is his status reduced in the community, but he can see little or no purpose for his life.

Meaningless leisure time. Not only was work the dominant factor in the lives of many persons who are now retired; it also consumed most of their waking hours. Many of them worked forty-eight, sixty, and even seventy hours a week during their active years. They had no time to learn how to enjoy reading, drama, music, art, sports, handicrafts. Hours hang heavy on their hands today.

Bereavement. Many aging persons have lost their dearest friends, life partners, and other relatives through death. While only 22.5 per cent of the men who are sixty-five and over in the United States are widowers, 55 per cent of the women of this age are widows.

Ill health. Chronic illness is four times as prevalent among persons sixty-five and over as it is among the population as a whole. Very little progress has been made against the chronic diseases that affect the old: vascular degeneration including hypertension, coronary, artery, and renal diseases; cancer; chronic bronchitis; diabetes; and mental disorder.

Inadequate preparation for the end of life. It is customary in our society to mention death as little as possible. We tend to think that if we refuse to recognize it, it will go away. We lack spiritual preparation for the end of our earthly existence, and many of us fail to make those decisions that would make life much easier for our survivors.

Inadequate housing. Some older people live in houses that are too large for them to maintain; many others cannot find adequate housing at prices they can afford. In many communities suitable housing is not available for persons at the various stages of the aging process.

WHICH PROBLEMS CAN CHURCHES HELP TO SOLVE?

Some of the traumatic situations that are the lot of the aging can be borne only in the fullness of Christian faith. How does one cope with the fact that his years of greatest vocational effectiveness are over, that his contributions from now on will be very limited? How does one "adjust" to the death of a life partner? How does one find meaning in a life that is stripped of most of its powers and capacities? Where else, but in the church? Older persons need to be *integrated into the life of a local church* that deals with the problems of life and death in the presence of God.

Elderly people have more free time than most others. Many of them lack the education and experience necessary for using leisure creatively. Frequently they require *a separate program designed to meet their needs.*

The aging have many problems that they cannot solve alone. They need the assistance of the *social service committee of the church.*

Some of the problems of the aging in the United States and Canada in such areas as employment practices, pension benefits, the financing of health care, and regulations concerning nursing homes cannot be solved without government action. Members of the church can get help on the fulfillment of their citizenship responsibilities on behalf of the aging from *the social education and action committee of the church.*

One of the ways to meet the needs of the aging for better housing and for care during illness is through *the agencies and institutions of the church.*

Let us consider what the churches are doing to make life more tolerable and interesting for the aging through each of the five channels suggested above.

INTEGRATION INTO THE WHOLE
LIFE OF THE CHURCH

Most of the denominations are deeply concerned about the problems of the aging. They are united in the belief that many of these problems can best be met in the life of the local church. Several denominations have prepared materials to help local churches fulfill their responsibilities toward the aging. Among these publications are: *The Congregation and the Older Adult*, National Lutheran Council; *Older Adults in the Church*, a manual, and *Mature Years*, a quarterly magazine for older people, The Methodist Church; *Aging: Today's Opportunities for the Church*, National Council of the Protestant Episcopal Church; *Older Persons in the Church Program*, United Presbyterian Church, U.S.A.; *Meeting The Fellowship Needs of Older Persons in the Local Church and the Community*, United Christian Missionary Society, Disciples of Christ; and *Churches and the Aging*, a packet of materials, Council for Christian Social Action, United Church of Christ.

The United Presbyterian Church, U.S.A., sought guidance for its work with the aging from the pastors of its synods and presbyteries. One of the questions asked was: "In the experience of your church do the majority of the older adults prefer: Segregation as an age group? Integration into the church's program without reference to age? A combination of both?"

Out of 795 replies, only 29 pastors thought that their

older adults wanted a segregated program; 476 thought they preferred integration in the whole program of the church; while 290 thought they preferred a combination of integrated and separate programs.

A number of local churches have held consultations on problems of the aging or have devoted a period of study to the subject. They have concluded that participation in the life of the whole church can be of great help to older adults in solving these problems: lack of purpose in life; meaningless leisure time; bereavement; and inadequate preparation for the end of life.

Finding renewed purpose for life. Older adults have found new or deeper meaning in life through participation in the services of worship, in Bible study, in discussions in the adult class, and in visits with the pastor and others. Services of worship have become more valuable as ministers have gained in understanding of the need of older adults to find deeper meaning for their lives. The sermon, the liturgy, and the sacraments have mediated the assurance that God loves all his children, regardless of age, and that he has a purpose for each of them.

Many older people have drifted away from the church and its practices. Some ministers have been aware of this situation and have given these persons special counsel concerning such elements of the Christian life as prayer, Bible study, and the sacraments.

The fellowship of the church has acquired a new dimension as members have sought to make old as well as young persons know that they are valued members of the Christian community.

Many churches have considered the infirmities of age as they installed loud speakers and special equipment for the hard of hearing. Others are now thinking of the needs of the aging as they erect new buildings or remodel present structures. Believing that facilities should be easily accessible for all types of older adults—those in wheel chairs, those with heart conditions, and others—they are eliminating door sills, and providing ramps at entrance doors and adding other features.

Using leisure time. One of the uses that elderly persons are finding for their leisure time is to give it to the church. Among the services that older adults are rendering in the local churches are:

Typing, mimeographing, addressing envelopes
Serving as receptionists
Cooking, serving meals
Baby-sitting on Sunday and during week-day meetings at the church
Telephoning, answering the phone
Visiting the sick and the housebound
Tutoring children
Making repairs in the homes of widows
Repairing clothing for needy members
Serving on church committees
Teaching in the church school
Helping members with legal problems

The work of many churches would have to be curtailed

drastically if the volunteer help of their senior citizens was withdrawn. Older members are often the most alert and helpful participants in study groups and other programs of the church.

Facing bereavement. It is estimated that the average person loses a family member or close friend approximately every ten years, but this experience comes to the older adult with more frequency. The fellowship of the church is often the most helpful factor in healing the wounds of bereavement.

Some churches have discovered that they can learn how to be more helpful to those who are bereaved. They have formed small committees to consider the pressing problems that many families confront when death occurs: buying the coffin; arranging for the funeral; settling the estate; planning living arrangements for the survivors. They know that families often spend far more money than they can afford for elaborate funerals, and they try to help them avoid this mistake. A committee sometimes arranges to have one of its members call on a family shortly after death occurs and offer its services. Such a committee in a Congregational church in Michigan has developed a flier that it distributes to its members, entitled "Suggestions Concerning Christian Funerals." A minister in Virginia has given his parishioners suggestions on "Writing Letters of Comfort."

The bereaved need the support of the Christian community during the long weeks and months that follow the death of a loved one. New friends and new groups gradually fill the gaping hole torn in the life of a bereaved person. Some of these new friends are found in the fellowship of the church.

Preparing for the end of life. Death may come for any person at any time. Those churches that deal with the ultimate issues of life and destiny are most helpful to their members as they prepare their spirits for entering the next phase of life.

Some churches encourage all their adult members to recognize the transitory nature of their own lives and to make three decisions that will be most helpful to their survivors. First is the disposition they wish made of their bodies. Do they want them buried? If so, where? Do they want them cremated? If so, what should be done with the ashes? Do they wish to give them to medical schools for research or to hospitals for the use that the living can make of eyes, heart, muscles, and other parts?

The second decision that a church member is asked to make is about the kind of funeral he prefers. Shall it be simple or elaborate? Should flowers be sent or the money donated to a memorial fund? Whom does he want to conduct the service?

The third decision concerns the division of property. Christians are asked to consider the needs of their families and dependents, and those of the church and other agencies and institutions of the larger community. They are urged to express their wishes in the legal form of a will.

Several churches in Cleveland, Ohio, encourage their

members to join the Cleveland Memorial Society. The purpose of the society is to enable families to provide simple, dignified funeral arrangements for the deceased. There are no regular dues. Families pay a $10 membership fee and fill out cards indicating the type of service desired in the event of the death of any family member. Members choose one of two types of service:

ONE: A funeral establishment to transport the body without embalming to a crematory where it will be cremated; the cost, including the price of cremation, not to exceed $200.

TWO: A funeral establishment to embalm the body if necessary, place it in a modest coffin, and arrange for a private burial before the memorial service; the cost not to exceed $300.

GROUP PROGRAMS FOR AGING PERSONS

Many older adults are delighted to take part in programs that churches design for them. There is considerable variety in the sponsorship of such groups and some diversity in the types of program that are offered. If there are enough older adults in one local church, it may sponsor the program. Sometimes several churches in one neighborhood combine forces to sponsor a program, but more often a neighborhood program is organized by the Council of Churches. Frequently, program activities for aging persons are organized by the city or by a community organization such as the YMCA, YWCA, or Salvation Army. The types of programs offered include fellowship meetings, recreation, arts and crafts, and conferences. There is great variety in the names chosen for clubs of aging persons: Gay Fellowship, Young at Heart, Happy Hours, Friendly Folks, Golden Age Club, Senior Citizens, Live Embers, Live Long and Like It Club, Plus Sixty Club, The Oldsters, the XYZ Club.

Let us see what some of our senior citizens are doing when they come together under church auspices:

St. Petersburg: an unofficial laboratory. St. Peter's Church (Episcopal) is in the center of St. Petersburg, Florida, where many elderly people go after retirement. Half of its communicants are more than sixty years old— there are eight hundred in the senior citizens' class, five hundred in the forty-one to sixty group, and three hundred in the eighteen to forty bracket. The rector and his three assistants have recognized their opportunity to experiment with parish work among the aging.

The chief problem that the older members of the church face is aloneness. Fourteen per cent of all St. Peter's men are widowed or single; and 66 per cent of the women over sixty are widowed or single. Most of those who are over sixty have no relatives in the city; in a crisis, they turn to the church.

St. Peter's has organized a series of discussion groups and lectures for its senior members, featuring such topics as "Adjustment to Retirement," "Problems of Bereavement," "Husband and Wife Relationships After Sixty," "Good Grooming," and "Acceptance of the Limitations of Age."

An occasional lecturer will speak and answer questions on a distinctly scholarly subject. An arts and crafts center, which will give older members a chance to learn and pursue hobbies, is in the blueprint stage.

Counseling aging members on romantic and moral problems is a part of a priest's duty at St. Peter's. Men and women who are left alone after years of marriage are often anxious to find other partners, and are not always wise in their choices. Laws that require women to relinquish income upon remarriage sometimes force desperately lonely widows into relationships that supply companionship but take a toll in guilt and uneasiness.

Christian education for the aging. Seventeen years ago, The Methodist Church recognized the need for a program of Christian education that would consider the relevance of the Christian faith to the problems faced by older persons. Miss Virginia Stafford was added to the staff of the Department of Christian Education for Adults and given the responsibility for work with the aging. A significant program has been developed that includes literature, workshops, and counsel with local churches. Miss Stafford reports that those churches that make a serious attempt to develop a Christian education program for the aging find that many of them are reclaimed for the Christian fellowship. Numerous persons in their seventies and beyond are joining the church on confession of faith.

Camping for older adults. Camping for senior citizens is becoming quite popular in both Canada and the United

States. Members of the UNITED CHURCH OF CANADA IN VANCOUVER go by steamship to a camp thirty miles away. They spend ten happy days in a program that combines worship, sports, crafts, and fellowship.

Senior men and women from the Episcopal Diocese of Ohio hold an annual conference at Kenyon College. They discuss the contributions that they can make to the church as well as the problems faced by the aging. The minister of a church that sends representatives to the conference each summer says, "A parish with a returned conferee has a burning fuse that can set off a chain reaction of interest and activity among its over sixty-fivers."

THE SOCIAL SERVICE COMMITTEE

Older persons who are in desperate need frequently do not know about the community resources that are available to them. Many churches serve as the vital link that connects the needy persons with the resources that can contribute to their economic security.

Even though the minister may know several of the older members of the congregation, most churches find it useful to make a survey of the aging and their needs. The Social Service Committee or a special committee appointed to work with older adults makes a systematic check on all the elderly members of the congregation. The committee gets their names and addresses, visits them in their homes, and makes a written record about each person. One visitor was amazed

68

to find these persons living within a one mile radius of the church:

Mrs. Holland, who sat alone in a one-room basement apartment. She did not dress or comb her hair, but sat wrapped in a little blanket—waiting for the visitor who came at last.

Mr. and Mrs. Bliss, who have been married many years and are still sweethearts. He is an invalid and over ninety; she has little vision, but manages to keep house for both of them.

Mrs. Lawler, who was a court reporter in her youth. She lives alone in a tiny house, but is so lonely she talks to herself in order not to forget the sound of a human voice.

The committee makes a summary of the number of older adults and their needs; it then sets out to find the resource groups in the community that can help these people. Frequently, the chief responsibility of the church is to refer the problem to the proper agency. Sometimes the church decides that it should meet the need with some direct action of its own.

Giving material assistance. The youth fellowship and the young adults are two groups within the church that frequently assume responsibility for giving aid to older people. Assistance is often given in a Work Day devoted to house-cleaning, painting, remodeling, repairing furniture and appliances. The Christianity in Action Program of Anderson College (Church of God) Anderson, Indiana, renders this kind of service to several families every year.

Visiting shut-ins. The Anglican Church of Canada, the United Lutheran Church in America, and other groups have prepared booklets to help church members become more helpful in visiting the sick and elderly. Among the many useful suggestions in the Lutheran booklet is this list that advises church callers about the attitudes and activities that will make their calls on shut ins as meaningful, beneficial, and effective as possible.

1. Be faithful.
2. Be a listener.
3. Be interested, patient, and cheerful.
4. Keep all confidences.
5. Plan your visits.
6. Witness to your own faith, but don't preach.
7. Be objective.
8. Be accepting.
9. Verify stories before reporting them to anyone; then only to the proper person.
10. Keep a notebook.
11. Remember birthdays and holidays with cards and small gifts.
12. Report to your pastor regularly and in writing.

Facilitating participation in worship. Many older persons can attend church services if someone takes them by car. Many churches ask families to "adopt" a grandparent and take him or her to church with them; many times the adopted grandparent goes home for Sunday dinner with the family. Ministers make the sacrament of communion available to older persons who are bedridden, whether in their own homes, nursing homes, or hospitals.

The Aging

Leaders in social education and action in the churches are concerned about five major problems of the aging: age as a basis for compulsory retirement, social security benefits, financing of health care, standards for nursing homes, and public housing.

Eliminating age restrictions on employment. It was once considered a commendable policy for the employer to require retirement at a specified age and to make provision for reduced incomes for retired workers. No one doubts the value of the provision of income for employees who are no longer able to work. Many people, however, question the wisdom of setting an arbitrary age at which retirement is mandatory. Some workers are forced to leave their positions when they would be able to render satisfactory service for five to ten more years. Many workers need employment during these years, and employers need their services. Some people believe that it is as unfair to discriminate against qualified persons on the basis of advanced age as it is to refuse to employ them because of race, sex, or nationality. When church members have discussed this question and have come to a consensus about it, they will be able to recommend action to employers and to the government.

Increasing pension benefits to retired workers. One of the reasons why the incomes of elderly persons are so inadequate is that their Social Security benefits are based on the low wages that they earned during their productive years. In August, 1959, Social Security (Old-age, Survivors, and Disability Insurance System) paid benefits to about nine and one-half million persons who were aged sixty-five or over. The monthly payments to retired workers averaged $72.46, or less than $900 per year. The average monthly payment to retired workers' wives or husbands was $38, or $456 per year. Since inflation has greatly increased the cost of what retired persons buy, many people believe that the United States Congress should increase the benefits paid to these pensioners.

THE COUNCIL FOR SOCIAL SERVICE of the Anglican Church of Canada is concerned about the financial situation of older persons. Between 40 and 60 per cent of the persons sixty and over in Ontario receive incomes that are too small to provide a "modest but adequate" standard of living. The council has recommended that Canada establish a contributory pension plan that would supplement the present universal rate of $55 per month paid to all persons over seventy years of age.

Financing medical care. Medical and hospital care has become increasingly expensive. The elderly, who can least afford this type of care, have greater need of it than persons of any other age group. One accident or severe illness may wipe out the life savings of an aged couple.

Many Christians feel that a way must be found to assist elderly persons to bear the cost of medical care. One step that has been taken is the establishment of a new program under the Old Age, Survivors, and Disability Insurance System (Social Security) that provides help for aged persons who are unable to pay their medical bills and that broadens disability protection. A health insurance program is still under consideration as this is written.

Raising the standards of nursing homes. Despite the great need for nursing homes, the conditions in many of them are so deplorable that physicians refuse to recommend them to their patients. Several social action committees are working in their states to see that the standards for sanitation, safety, and nursing care are more clearly defined by the authorities.

Providing public housing for the elderly. Housing at prices they can afford is a paramount need of the elderly. Several public housing projects have been required by law to maintain a certain percentage of units (often 10 per cent) for persons who are 65 or over. Other projects have been built exclusively for the aging. Social action committees will need to study this issue before recommending action to the government.

AGENCIES AND INSTITUTIONS

Local churches not only carry heavy responsibilities for the care of the aging; they also co-operate in the maintenance of many agencies and institutions for this purpose. Most of these agencies are concerned with housing, but others provide counseling service and give guidance to local churches on their programs for the elderly. In addition, many of the community centers maintained by American Baptists, Lutherans, Methodists, and other denominational groups include Golden Age Clubs or similar programs for the elderly.

Let us look at each of the types of service rendered by church agencies and institutions to older adults.

Guidance to churches. The National Council of the Protestant Episcopal Church has added a staff member to its Division of Health and Welfare Services who will carry responsibility for programs and ministries to the aging. He will give information and guidance to parish leaders who are developing programs for the aging; he will also give counsel to the agencies and institutions of the church that are at work in this field.

Counseling service for the aging. At least three denominations are experimenting with the employment of counselors who serve the aging in one geographical area:

UNITED PRESBYTERIAN CHURCH, U.S.A. The Presbytery of Westchester County, New York, has employed a community worker and given her a roving assignment to help meet the needs of the aging. Any minister can ask for her assistance. For instance, if a young couple has an aged parent living in the house and friction is developing, the worker might look for a community center where the older person could spend a portion of each day. The worker knows about medical care and welfare services and can refer the aging to them.

AMERICAN LUTHERAN CHURCH. The Lutheran Welfare Service of Southern California employs a deaconess who specializes in caring for older people. She finds places for them to live and gives them counsel about other problems.

PROTESTANT EPISCOPAL CHURCH. The Social Relations Department of the diocese of Washington, D.C., has established a series of Super-Sixties Clubs that are useful in locating those aging persons who need individual help; professional workers and trained volunteers then give counsel and aid.

Homes for the aging. Church groups are building more homes for the aging than any other type of institution. So many new homes are being built that it is almost impossible to make an accurate listing of their number. At least 569 agencies and homes are maintained by eleven denominations as follows:

American Baptist	54
Disciples of Christ	18
Evangelical United Brethren	9
Lutheran	165
Methodist	104
Moravian	5
Protestant Espicopal	73
Presbyterian, U.S.	13
Reformed Church in America	1
United Church of Canada	18
United Church of Christ	30
United Presbyterian, U.S.A.	79

Byron Johnson, formerly a member of the United States House of Representatives, has described the four types of housing that are required to meet the varied needs of men and women who are elderly.

Mr. Johnson, in a magazine article, said:

We tend to speak of "homes for the aging" as though there were one type of housing that would meet the wide range of needs of elderly persons. Actually, four very different types of housing and care are required to meet the needs of persons at various stages of the aging process:

HOUSING FOR LATER MATURITY. Most people at this period of their lives can take care of themselves but they need smaller units at prices they can afford. This type of housing can be built for $6,500 and up per unit.

HOUSEKEEPING CARE. Many people can dress themselves, feed themselves, and look after their own physical needs, but the physical labor of housekeeping is beyond their strength. They need meals and maid service, which may be rendered in their own homes or in a housing project.

NURSING CARE. Persons who are infirm but not ill need medical aid and nursing care on a continuing basis. Perhaps 3 per cent of the aged need this type of help. It may be given in private residences or in nursing homes. It costs from $9,000 to $14,000 per bed to build a nursing home and from $9 to $15 per bed per day to operate it.

HOSPITALIZATION. At any given time perhaps 3 per cent of the aged may be seriously ill. They need to be in hospitals where medical services are available to restore them to health or to ease their pain. It costs from $15,000 to $30,000 per bed to build a hospital and from $15 to $30 per day to operate it. Obviously, we cannot afford to maintain elderly persons in hospitals when all they need is minimal nursing care or house-keeping services.[1]

What type of housing needs are church homes for the aging designed to meet? Most of them are planned to provide care for persons in late maturity, some of them provide nursing care, and a few are prepared to offer both types of care.

There is wide variety in the costs that residents are asked to pay in church homes. Some are built to meet the needs of the 50 per cent of the aging who live on $1,200 per year or less, but others charge fees that only a few can afford. Some homes require a "down payment" of from $1,000 to $15,000 and charge monthly rates of from $100 to $400. Old-age Assistance, given to needy elderly persons under the Social Security Act, is a boon to those who need the care of such homes but do not have sufficient funds of their own to meet the cost for services. Many homes admit persons who receive Old-age Assistance. No home operated by the former Evangelical and Reformed Church (now a part of the United Church of Christ) has ever refused admission to an elderly person because of lack of funds.

The cottage plan. Some denominations are building communities for aged individuals and couples. For instance, the OKLAHOMA CHRISTIAN HOME (Disciples of Christ) in Edmond, Oklahoma, has developed a plan whereby couples and individuals can build houses on the grounds of the

[1] "Housing for Senior Citizens," by Byron Johnson, in *Social Action,* January, 1960, pp. 16-17. Used by permission.

home. Each house is built according to the plans of its donor and first resident, but it becomes the property of the Oklahoma Christian Home. A contract is made that gives the builder the right to live in the cottage as long as he lives and is able to care for himself. When he is no longer capable of self care he is moved into the main building and cared for as long as he lives. Occupants of the cottages have the advantage of living independently yet being able to participate in the activities of the home. A similar community for senior citizens is being planned by the Council of Churches in Oklahoma City.

Non resident care—a casework service. Many homes have long waiting lists of persons seeking entrance. Some of them employ a caseworker who keeps in touch with these persons and helps them solve some of their problems in their present environment. This type of service enables the home to serve more people than can be housed inside its walls and to become acquainted with some of its future residents.

Foster home care. Churches in the United States and Canada are experimenting with the placement of older persons in foster homes, where fellowship with their friends can be continued. Leonard F. Hatfield, general secretary of the COUNCIL FOR SOCIAL SERVICE of the Anglican Church of Canada, describes one such placement:

At eighty-nine, Mrs. Brown is a spry, bright-eyed woman who can knit a pair of socks a day without glasses, is interested in what goes on around her, and travels alone by bus, subway, and streetcar every Sunday morning to church. The father of the family with whom she is living works on a night shift, which means that Mrs. Brown is great company for his wife during the evening. She is so happy to be living where she can visit all her old friends again, but perhaps it is the children who make the most difference. They call her "Granny" and fight for the honor of calling her to dinner. "They seem to like me," she says, "and for that alone it is worth staying." [1]

EVALUATION OF WORK WITH
THE AGING

Older adults have many problems that can best be met by partaking of the depth and richness of the life of the Christian church. They have other problems that call for assistance from the social service and social action committees of local churches. Some churches have given careful consideration to the problems of the aging and have altered their programs so as to serve them more effectively. Unfortunately, the majority have given little thought to this significant group of people.

Churches are devoting most of their time and resources to meeting the needs of the elderly for adequate housing—to the neglect of other needs. They tend to make one response to the need for housing: to build homes for the able-bodied adults in late maturity. This decision raises many questions with which churches will be wrestling in the decade ahead. Among them are: Is it advisable for an able-

[1] Hatfield, Leonard F. *He Cares.* Toronto, Canada: The Anglican Church of Canada, 1959. Used by permission.

bodied older person to break ties with his home community and live in an institutional home that may be in another city or neighborhood? Do church homes serve aging persons at all income levels or do they benefit principally those in the middle and upper income brackets? What proportion of them serve the 50 per cent of the aging who have per capita incomes of less than $1,200 per year? Should the churches devote more of their resources to providing counselors to the aging who can help them meet their needs in their own homes? Should the churches take greater responsibility for meeting the desperate need for adequate nursing care? If so, should they establish new nursing homes or should they encourage government and private agencies to do so; and devote their major energies to obtaining better standards of operation, providing chaplaincy service, and rendering volunteer assistance?

It is hoped that in the decade ahead far more churches will give compassionate and creative attention to meeting the needs of the aging.

CHAPTER FIVE

The Physically Ill, the Mentally Ill, the Handicapped

And he went about all Galilee, teaching in their synagogues and preaching the gospel of the kingdom and
healing every disease and every infirmity among the
people. —Matthew 4:23.

The concern of Christians for the physically ill, the mentally ill, and the handicapped is a direct outgrowth of the
healing ministry of Jesus Christ. The gospels give accounts
of twenty-six times when Jesus healed one or more persons.
Among the conditions that he healed were blindness,
paralysis, the possession by demons, leprosy, fever, lameness,
hemorrhaging, deafness, epilepsy, and dropsy.

Why did Jesus include healing in his ministry? The gospels refer to his healing as though it were a normal part
of the work of one who lived close to God. Only occasionally is a reason given for his healing, and it is usually compassion: Jesus had pity on the two blind men on the road
from Jericho (Matthew 20:30-34); he had compassion on
the widow whose only son had died (Luke 7:11-15). Jesus
knew that it is God's will that every man be whole. Health

is not only desirable in itself, but it also enables men to serve God more fully.

THE RELATION OF CHRISTIAN FAITH TO HEALTH

Throughout most of human history there has been a close relationship between religion and healing. The medicine man of the primitive tribe was also a religious leader. The medical practitioners of ancient Egypt were the priests, As was seen in chapter two, the Christian church has ministered to the sick throughout its history

With the rise of modern scientific medicine, there came a rift between physician and pastor. Medicine became almost completely secularized, despite the fact that churches continued to maintain hospitals. The result of this separation was that medicine tended to become materialistic and lose sight of the spiritual dimension of health.

Fortunately, ministers and physicians, medicine and religion, are coming to a better understanding of each other. Physicians are recognizing the emotional causes of disease and the part that faith can play in its cure. Ministers are more conscious of the scientific aspects of medicine and seek to co-operate with doctors. With the exception of a few sects that rely wholly on faith healing, the churches expect that their healing ministries will draw upon all the resources of modern scientific medicine *and* faith. They recognize that God is the source of all healing, including the scientific processes used by physicians.

The Physically Ill, the Mentally Ill, the Handicapped

A great contribution to better understanding between religion and medicine has been made by the United Presbyterian Church, U.S.A. A committee composed of ministers, physicians, psychologists, and professors studied the contributions that science and religion can make to healing. One result of the study was a remarkable booklet called *The Relation of Christian Faith to Health.*[1] It considers the relation of Christian faith to health in New Testament times and today. It then analyzes the contributions that physicians, pastors, and Christian laymen can make in healing the sick and suggests that they work in close co-operation with one another. This booklet is proving useful as a basis for discussion between pastors and physicians.

THE HEALING MINISTRY OF
CHURCHES TODAY

The Protestant churches of Canada and the United States maintain a vast network of agencies, institutions, and services devoted to healing. Some evidence of the healing ministries of the churches has been seen in chapters three and four. The churches make these further contributions: the maintenance of institutions for healing the physically ill and the mentally ill and for the rehabilitation of the handicapped; the giving of Christian service in private and government hospitals through chaplains and volunteer workers; the training of physicians, nurses, and other professional

[1] *The Relation of Christian Faith to Health,* Adopted by the 172nd General Assembly, United Presbyterian Church, U.S.A., May, 1960.

workers; and the development of public opinion on health problems through programs of education and action. Let us consider each of the major contributions that churches make through their healing ministries.

THE CHURCHES SERVE THE
PHYSICALLY ILL

Churches have made a significant contribution to the development of the health services of Canada and the United States. Churches were responsible for the establishment of many hospitals during the nineteenth century. While they have built many new healing institutions during the twentieth century, private agencies and the government have built far more and larger ones.

The number of Protestant institutions. An impressive number of hospitals, clinics, convalescent homes, and dispensaries are related to Protestant churches. Some of these institutions serve scattered populations in remote rural areas; others are world-famous hospitals in great cities, such as the Columbia Presbyterian Medical Center in New York, Wesley Memorial Hospital in Chicago, and St. Luke's Hospital (Episcopal) in New York.

Here is a brief listing of the types of healing agencies related to Protestant denominations in Canada and the United States:

American Baptist Convention—7 hospitals
Anglican Church of Canada—7 hospitals, 2 convalescent homes, and 2 mission ships whose two-way radio telephones enable

them to hear calls of distress and treat the sick and injured in their isolated homes or transport them to the nearest hospital

Church of the Brethren—1 hospital in Chicago, 6 hospitals in Puerto Rico

Evangelical United Brethren—3 hospitals

Lutheran Churches—125 general hospitals, 2 tuberculosis sanitaria, and 10 institutions serving the physically or mentally handicapped

The Methodist Church—83 hospitals, 7 of which are operated under the direction of The Woman's Division of Christian Service

Protestant Episcopal Church—58 hospitals and 12 convalescent homes

United Church of Canada—17 hospitals

United Church of Christ—11 hospitals and 4 convalescent or nursing homes

United Presbyterian Church, U.S.A.—23 hospitals, 9 nursing homes, and 17 out-patient clinics

What share of the load do church-related hospitals carry? It is impossible to give a precise answer concerning the proportionate share of the total responsibility for health services borne by church-related hospitals. The information available does not separate the contribution made by Protestant, Roman Catholic, Jewish, and other church-related hospitals. The table on the following page sheds some light on the services rendered by various types of hospitals in the United States in 1960:[1]

[1] Reprinted with permission from Guide Issue of *Hospitals,* Journal of the American Hospital Association, 35:398, 400, August 1, 1961 (Part Two).

	Number of Hospitals	Number of Beds	Number of Patients Admitted
GOVERNMENTAL:			
Federal	435	177,105	1,475,530
State	556	752,148	929,849
County	749	111,271	1,985,154
City	350	65,828	1,361,799
City-County	82	12,787	381,834
Hospital District	143	11,436	406,421
Governmental Totals	2,315	1,130,575	6,540,587
NON-GOVERNMENTAL:			
Church	1,241	192,743	7,152,418
Other Voluntary	2,338	288,843	9,735,751
Proprietary	982	45,809	1,598,406
Non-governmental Totals	4,561	527,395	18,486,565
Totals for the United States	6,876	1,657,970	25,027,152

These figures indicate that the 1,241 hospitals related to *all* religious groups constituted not quite one fifth of the total number of hospitals in the United States in 1960; religious bodies maintained less than one eighth of all the hospital beds; and they served more than one fourth of all patients admitted to hospitals that year.

Many of the beds in government hospitals are occupied by veterans and by patients suffering from mental difficulties, tuberculosis, and other problems that require treatment for several months or years. Most of the hospitals related to churches are general hospitals where the average length of stay is 8.4 days (United States average for short-term stays during 1959.)

The United States needs more hospital facilities. Very few hospitals were built from the depth of the depression in 1933 until after the end of World War II in 1945. Although many hospitals have been built since then, it is estimated that the United States needs 855,000 more hospital beds now, and that by 1985 it will need one new bed for every one that was in use in 1959—or 1,612,822 more. This figure is based on present need plus the anticipated growth in the population.[1]

The greatest needs for additional health facilities are in four fields, according to Dr. Jack Haldeman, deputy surgeon general of the United States Public Health Service. These are: first, in the rural areas where two and one half million persons are without hospital facilities; second, for patients needing long-term care for chronic diseases; third, in urban areas where obsolescent plants make health care inadequate; and fourth, for persons who are mentally ill.

The estimated average cost of building and equipping hospitals is $18,000 per bed. It would cost 16 billion dollars to supply the 855,000 hospital beds needed now. How many of these beds will be furnished by agencies of the Protestant churches?

Relationship to the churches. Hospitals are less closely related to church bodies than are other institutions of social

---

[1] *The Federal Budget and the General Welfare,* Conference on Economic Progress, 1001 Connecticut Avenue, N.W., Washington 6, D.C.

welfare. The relationship ranges from those that are owned and operated by a church body to those that are actually independent but maintain some token relationship. Of the twenty-three hospitals related to the United Presbyterian Church, U.S.A., five are directly owned and operated; two are operated by a board that is controlled by a judicatory; ten are operated by a board related to a judicatory; three are operated by a board related to individual churches, and three are independent. A report of a Presbyterian study committee states that "the three so-called 'independent' are the Presbyterian hospitals in New York, Newark, and Pittsburgh. All enjoy some kind of relationship to the church but are not legally tied to it."

The relationship of a hospital to a church body is indicated partly by the source of its income. Olin E. Oeschger, general secretary of the Board of Hospitals and Homes of The Methodist Church, reported in 1961: "There are 76 general hospitals in the United States affiliated with this Board. . . . Thirty of our affiliated hospitals received nothing from the church for operating expenses; 18 received less than $5,000. The total amount received constituted only 8.8 per cent of the free and part-pay services rendered."

The report of the Presbyterian study committee indicated that the churches' hospitals have come to the place where "virtually all support comes from fees for services rendered, relieving the church constituency of the burden of paying for people who can pay for themselves and freeing church benevolences for the extension of existing services,

the opening of new ones, and the care of the medically in-
digent."

The sources of income for hospitals related to Protestant
denominations was indicated by a study made by the National Council of Churches in 1954. The hospitals surveyed
reported that 92.2 per cent of their income came from fees
and investments; 8 per cent was contributed by individuals;
4.8 per cent came from Community Chests; 1.1 per cent
came from other sources; while only 17 per cent was contributed by religious bodies.

Medical units of mission stations. Many of the medical
services of the churches are conducted in connection with
their missions in rural areas. Some indication of the type of
work done and the need for it is indicated by this excerpt
from the diary of the doctor related to Mora Valley Medical Unit (Presbyterian) in a remote section of New Mexico.

Frequently we are interrupted in the midst of our morning
devotions by the doorbell. As we go to the door, we may see
several pick-ups, perhaps a horse and wagon, and even some
fine-looking family cars lined up waiting the 9 A.M. hour. Our
first case is an emergency—a boy with an ugly stab wound. All
goes smoothly for an hour or so until a request comes in for a
home call to see someone who has "fainted and cannot be
moved." Doctor and nurse take off to give emergency care to an
elderly lady who has had a stroke and whose condition is poor.
Back to the clinic . . . ten more patients before lunch. We
sit down with a sigh of relief to enjoy a rest. BZZZ! This time
it's the deputy sheriff and another emergency away up in a

high mountain valley. "Hurry! A man has been shot." So we hurry, glad to be able to bring comfort and relief to people who never before even sought medical care.[1]

THE CHURCHES SERVE THE MENTALLY ILL

There are scores of different mental disorders or illnesses, some of which are quite mild and others severe. Most of them can be divided into two major groups: psychoses and neuroses. Psychoses are the mental illnesses that have been known as "insanity." The behavior of a psychotic person is irrational because he has lost touch with reality. The largest group of mental illnesses are the neuroses, in which the affected persons retain contact with reality, but have an inaccurate concept of it.

Great strides are being made in healing persons who suffer from mental illness. For many persons, the period of treatment is quite long, although some of the new drugs are making it possible to shorten the process.

How prevalent is mental illness?   On an average day in 1959 a census-taker would have found 1,363,217 patients in hospitals around the United States; and more than half of them, or 707,769, would have been suffering from mental illnesses. While it is true that more than half of all hospital beds are occupied by mental patients, it is not true that half of those who enter hospitals are mental patients. The aver-

[1] Harrington, Janette T. and Hermann, Mildred M. *Encounter with Crisis*, p. 111. New York: Board of National Missions, United Presbyterian Church in the U.S.A., 1960. Used by permission.

age length of stay in a mental hospital is nearly three years, while the average length of stay in the hospital for a short-term illness in 1959 was, as mentioned earlier, 8.4 days. We can gain clearer insight into the proportion of the sick who are suffering from mental illness by considering the number of persons admitted to hospitals. In 1959, 23,605,-186 patients were admitted to all hospitals in the United States; 400,370 of this number—only a fraction of the whole—were admitted for psychiatric treatment.

The situation is similar in Canada. Mental illness is the country's number one health problem. At least one million Canadians, or one in every sixteen, are suffering from some form of mental disability. About seventy thousand persons are in mental hospitals; about twenty thousand new patients are admitted each year.

About 30 per cent of all persons admitted to mental hospitals each year are elderly persons suffering from the psychoses of old age: primarily cerebral arteriosclerosis or senile psychosis. The majority of them die within a year or two.

About 90 per cent of all persons who enter institutions to receive treatment or custodial care for mental illness go to hospitals operated by state governments. There are also several hundred private mental hospitals that are quite small. Some of these are operated for profit, and the cost may be from $25 to $50 per day.

How do churches serve the mentally ill? The contribution that churches make to the treatment of the mentally ill is in sharp contrast to that which they make to persons who are physically sick. While more than one fourth of all persons who were admitted to hospitals in 1959 entered church-related institutions, most of them went for the treatment of physical illness. Church-related institutions treat only a very small percentage of the mental patients of the country. One or two denominations maintain agencies and institutions devoted to the healing of mental illness, but the greatest contribution is made by local churches through pastoral counseling and rehabilitation of patients released from mental hospitals. Most denominations help to maintain chaplains in mental hospitals, as they do in other healing institutions. Let us consider these contributions in sufficient detail to define them clearly.

Institutions of healing. THE FRIENDS were among the first to discover that an insane person was ill, rather than evil. The best known forerunner of modern institutions was the York Retreat, which was started by William Tuke in 1792 and which still continues its service. Many Friends have been among the leaders of the mental health movement in this century.

THE LUTHERAN CHURCHES. A number of general hospitals are developing services for the mentally ill, either for patients in residence or in out-patient clinics. Lutheran Medical Center, Brooklyn, New York, for example, operates an out-patient clinic, while Fairview Hospital in Minneapolis, Minnesota, has established a department for the treatment of the mentally ill patients in residence.

THE REFORMED CHURCH IN AMERICA co-operates with

other churches in the support of Pine Rest Sanitarium in Grand Rapids, Michigan; the Bethesda Sanitarium in Denver, Colorado; and the Christian Sanitarium in Wyckoff, New Jersey.

MENNONITES. The first mental hospital established by the Mennonite Central Committee grew out of the experience of its conscientious objectors who did their alternate service in state mental hospitals during World War II. These young men were shocked by the conditions they found in the state hospitals: little therapy, too many patients in proportion to the number of staff members, lack of patience and loving care. When they completed their years of service they urged the denomination to establish mental hospitals. The first one, Brook Lane Farm, was begun at Hagerstown, Maryland, in 1949. Two others are now in operation and a fourth is under construction. Each hospital is small, serving about forty persons, and the staff is relatively large—about forty persons. There has been some soul-searching among church leaders as to whether the denomination should "perform a community service that secular society can do just as well," but the decision has been that the church should develop a program that meets standards of professional excellence and is "uniquely and constructively expressive of Christ's spirit."

The problem of finance is a perplexing one to the Mennonites. Their mental hospitals are expected to be self-supporting. The costs are relatively low—for maintenance and professional services the costs are $15 to $28 per day.

But the question persists as to what the hospitals should do about persons who need help but are unable to pay for it.

Mental health clinics. Several local churches have developed mental health clinics that provide psychological counseling and therapy for members of the church and community. One notable example is the Mental Hygiene Clinic developed by the Church of the Master (Presbyterian) in the Harlem area of New York. It served 2,400 patients in 1959.

Rehabilitation of former patients. Several denominations, among them the Church of the Brethren and the United Church of Christ, have programs in which local churches receive patients who are released from mental hospitals and help them reestablish themselves in the community. The Council of Churches in Minneapolis, Minnesota, has established a social rehabilitation center for patients who have undergone treatment for mental illness. Volunteers from United Church Women work with professional staff members in a program designed to help these people adjust to normal community living.

A new trend in the rehabilitation of the mentally ill is to send them out into the community for short periods after they have begun to show improvement. Groups of church women have been helpful in this process. After careful training, they offer hospitality to such patients, first for afternoon drives or luncheons, and later for weekends. The women of St. John's Church, Episcopal, in Northampton, Massachusetts, started such a program ten years ago. Beginning with a small unit in the nearby State Hospital, this volunteer service now involves all the churches of the city and serves several institutions.

Pastoral counseling. Many pastors have helped church members avert serious mental illness through counseling and by referring them to physicians. They have also helped families adjust to the mental illness of a member and learn how to cope with it. Many theological seminaries are now giving students specialized training in pastoral counseling of the mentally ill and their families.

THE CHURCHES SERVE THE
PHYSICALLY HANDICAPPED

Do persons with physical handicaps feel welcome in local churches? Do they participate fully in their programs? The American Baptist Home Mission Societies asked ministers these questions. The replies from 380 churches indicated that persons with a wide variety of handicaps take part in the life of these churches, but that their proportion in the church is considerably smaller than in the population as a whole. Perhaps not enough effort is given to making them feel at ease in churches.

Let us consider some agencies of the churches that are helping to aid three groups of physically handicapped persons: the mentally retarded, the blind, and the deaf.

Care for the mentally retarded. THE VILLAGE OF EMMAUS is a home for mentally retarded women and girls, at St. Charles, Missouri, which is maintained by the United

Church of Christ. Most of the more than two hundred residents cannot be trained for life in a normal community, but they live with satisfaction in this sheltered community. The superintendent introduces some of the residents:

Carla has been at Emmaus for thirty-two years. One of her assignments is to feed Martha, a helpless child. Carla used to wonder if she would ever be well enough to leave Emmaus. Now she is content to stay and take care of Martha.

Susan and Doris spend happy hours together sharing their toys as they play on the floor. Each has the mentality of a three year old, but Susan is five and Doris is twenty-seven.

Aid for the blind More than 350,000 persons in Canada and the United States are blind—one in every five hundred persons in the population. Some were born blind and have never known what it means to see. Others can tell light from dark and some are even able to read large print. While a few are young, the majority are over sixty years of age.

Church-related hospitals do their part in seeking to prevent blindness. One example of outstanding work is that done by the Wolff Eye Clinic in the Evangelical and Reformed Hospital, Marshalltown, Iowa. Most of the work that churches are doing to assist persons who are blind is done on an interdenominational basis, through two agencies:

THE AMERICAN BIBLE SOCIETY feels responsible for producing the Bible and sections of it in many languages and in whatever form is necessary. It aids the blind by producing Bibles in braille and making spoken LP records of scripture. Its charter prevents the society from publishing any comments on the Bible.

THE JOHN MILTON SOCIETY, named in honor of the blind poet, was organized in 1929 for the purpose of making Christian literature, other than the Bible, available to the blind. It works on behalf of sixty Protestant denominations and is related to those divisions of the National Council of Churches that are responsible for Christian education, home missions, and foreign missions.

The society produces a wide variety of materials that are sent free to blind persons anywhere, on request to its headquarters, at 475 Riverside Drive, New York 27, New York. It publishes three magazines: the *John Milton Magazine* (monthly), the *John Milton Sunday School Quarterly* in braille for adult readers-by-touch, and a children's magazine called *Discovery*. It is estimated that only about one fourth of the blind in Canada and the United States read braille; consequently the society "publishes" the *John Milton Talking Book Magazine* on records and produces and distributes the *John Milton Recorded Sunday School Lessons*.

The John Milton Society also publishes materials that interpret blindness to sighted persons and gives suggestions to them for dealing with the blind. One pamphlet dispels some notions about blindness that are widespread. It reminds us that:

Blindness is not a crippling handicap. Many regard their blindness as a sort of inconvenience and ignore it as much as possible—going on to win distinction in many fields.

Blindness does not automatically develop other senses. Blind persons, having to rely on their other senses, train themselves to note the sound and feel, the taste and smell of things most people overlook.

Blindness does not make people alike. "The blind," as a separate people, do not exist; happening to be blind, they may otherwise be quite dissimilar.

Blindness need not mean darkness. Since life seems light or dark according to inner radiance rather than physical sight, some blind people help those with normal eyesight see life more slowly and surely.

Religious experience for the deaf. A survey conducted in 1952 revealed that about 10 per cent of the population of the United States have some impairment of hearing, and that 2.4 per cent of the children are handicapped by a serious amount of impairment or by total deafness. Communication is very difficult for the totally deaf. They use the sign language or lip-reading or a combination of the two—but none of these methods permits the transmission of more than limited meanings.

There are a few congregations, of various denominations, composed of deaf persons. Among them are the Church of the Deaf (Methodist) in Cincinnati, Ohio; Christ Methodist Church for the Deaf, Baltimore, Maryland; Ephphatha Church (Lutheran), Faribault, Minnesota; and Bread of Life Lutheran Church, Minneapolis, Minnesota. In addition, several local churches have separate worship services and church school programs for their deaf members. The Methodists in Southern Illinois conducted a two-day camp meeting for the deaf at Little Grassy Methodist Camp; the program combined some of the features of modern camping and an old-fashioned evangelistic tent meeting.

The Protestant Episcopal Church, which has done pioneering work with the deaf, is developing a national program that will produce Christian education materials for use with the deaf. It also encourages all clergymen to learn enough of the sign language to have some communication with the deaf. The church has appointed a chaplain to the only college for the deaf in the United States, Gallaudet, in Washington, D.C.

EDUCATION OF DOCTORS, NURSES, AND OTHER HEALTH WORKERS

There is an urgent need for more physicians, nurses, and other health workers in Canada and the United States. The Surgeon General's Consultant Group on Medical Education says that the United States must retain its ratio of 141 physicians per one hundred thousand of the population if it is to protect the health of its people. To maintain this standard, the number of physicians graduated annually must be increased from 7,400 a year to 11,000 by 1975. This is an increase of 3,600 graduates a year. Even though there are more nurses in the United States now than ever before—450,000—it is estimated that 140,000 additional nurses are needed and that the need will increase. There is also a great shortage in the number of other health workers who are needed on today's medical team: radiologists, social workers, chaplains, physical therapists, pharmacists, medical technologists, X-ray technicians, and others.

What are church-related hospitals doing to train doctors, nurses, and related health workers? The Methodist Church reports that forty-five of the seventy-six hospitals operated by its Board of Hospitals and Homes are conducting schools of nursing and that thirty-nine of them offer some of the training necessary for physicians. The hospitals of other denominations are also helping to train some of the professional workers who will be needed.

CHAPLAINCY SERVICE

Professionally trained chaplains are now recognized as essential members of the healing team in most general and mental hospitals. In many cases the chaplains are employed by the hospital, but in others they are maintained by local churches, councils of churches, or national mission boards. Regardless of who employs the chaplain, he is closely related to the chaplaincy service of his denomination and the American Protestant Hospital Chaplains' Association.

Clinical training for chaplains. A professionally trained chaplain is an ordained minister who has had at least six months of clinical training in a hospital or other institution, in addition to his theological studies. The chaplain may have taken this training shortly after graduation from seminary or he may have taken it after spending several years in the pastorate. Clinical training is co-ordinated by the Council for Clinical Training, 475 Riverside Drive, New York 27, N.Y.; it is given in more than fifty-five hospitals and other institutions throughout the United States.

The chaplain's contribution. The chaplain of a hospital works in close co-operation with the physicians and nurses; he also works with the patients' pastors. Pastors may be able to give the chaplain information that enables him to be more effective as he talks with patients day by day. The story of John Langley illustrates how chaplains can help restore to wholeness a person who is divided within himself; it also illustrates fruitful co-operation between two chaplains.

John Langley was admitted to Bellevue Hospital for observation. Doctors found him beating his head against the wall. "I'm not sick; I shouldn't be here," he told the doctors, and refused to tell them the reasons for his extreme depression.

When the chaplain first visited him, John swung around on the bench and faced the wall. He said, "Leave me alone." The chaplain, knowing that often the patients who are most hostile are the ones who really desire his counsel, sat down and waited quietly. Finally, John asked him, "Do you have anything better to do than sit here with me?" The answer was, "No, certainly not." After a long pause, the silence was broken by John, who said that no one really cared what happened to him. His wife had been dead for many years and his two married daughters never wrote or visited him. The chaplain assured him that he and the doctors cared and wanted to help him. John finally decided to co-operate with the staff. In subsequent visits the chaplain learned that John Langley had been confirmed in the Protestant Episcopal Church but had not attended worship for many years. The chaplain reminded him of God's love for him. He said, "If you will let him, God will help you get well."

A month later John was sent to Rockland State Hospital for treatment, but he was not frightened. He had a friend, and he knew he needed the help that was offered. The chaplain at Bellevue wrote to the Episcopal chaplain at Rockland and sent him records of John's spiritual progress. On Sunday, John attended worship in the auditorium and afterward talked with the priest. Arrangements were made for weekly visits. Eventually he was restored to health and to participation in the church.[1]

One other story indicates the great contribution that hospital chaplains make. A Presbyterian chaplain in the Los Angeles County General Hospital tells of this experience:

In the cancer ward, I met for the first time a once-beautiful Presbyterian woman of forty-one. Without any preliminaries, she said, "Tell me, what is death like? I don't think I'll be afraid of it. But the nearer it comes, the less sure I am."

For the next few minutes, and on four subsequent visits, I prayed with her and took her to the 23rd Psalm, the 14th chapter of John, and other passages and inspirational poems. Eighteen days later she faced the test we had discussed. I felt quite sure she faced it unafraid.[2]

[1] Adapted from "Behind the Barricade," by Shelby Moorman, in *Forth*, for September, 1959, p. 12. Used by permission.
[2] Harrington and Hermann, *op. cit.*, pp. 113-114. Used by permission.

CHURCH MEMBERS RENDER
VOLUNTEER SERVICE

Church members contribute millions of hours of service each year to patients in hospitals; among the people who render these services are: high school and college students who give their summer vacations; young men who are conscientious objectors to war and give their time as an alternative to military service; and adult volunteers who perform a myriad of invaluable services. Let us look briefly at the contributions of each group.

High school and college students. Several thousand American students have discovered that it is more exciting to give their services through a summer work camp than to loaf or hold a paid job. They participate in the hundred or more work projects sponsored by the denominations, the Student YMCA and YWCA, and other agencies. One example of this type of work is the service given by a group of Protestant Episcopal students as orderlies and nurses' aids in Norton Memorial Hospital, Louisville, Kentucky. They not only rendered a great service to the patients; they also gained a comprehensive view of the work of hospitals.

Conscientious objectors. A small but significant group of young men are conscientious objectors to war. Instead of performing eighteen months of military service, they contribute these months to the agencies and institutions of the churches. This form of alternative service is recognized by the government. Many conscientious objectors serve as orderlies in general hospitals and as guards in mental hospitals. Among the denominational groups that direct this type of work for young men are the Friends, the Mennonites, the Methodists, and the Brethren.

Adult volunteers. The third type of contributed service is that rendered by adult volunteers. Members of the women's fellowship of the denominations and of United Church Women give hundreds of thousands of hours of work per month to the sick in hospitals. Volunteers show patients to their rooms when they enter the hospital, bring magazines and books to their bedsides, visit with them, and run errands for them. The Methodist Church estimates that 25,000 persons a year render volunteer service in its hospitals alone. Since volunteers do not confine their services to denominational hospitals but serve in those operated by private and government agencies as well, the total number of volunteers must be very large indeed. Episcopalians of Oregon make regular visits to hospitals and nursing homes; and several Protestant Episcopal churches have "adopted" wards in mental hospitals, taking special responsibility for the eighty women in each of them.

So many members of the United Church of Canada volunteer their services in hospitals that the Board of Evangelism and Social Service has prepared a leaflet giving them suggestions concerning the performances of their tasks. The National Association for Mental Health discovered that many mental hospitals have recently added directors of volunteer services to their staffs. Since many of them had little experience in this new field, the National Association conducted a nationwide institute to enable them to share experiences with one another.

One of the most important groups of volunteers are those men and women who serve on the boards of hospitals. They are the ones who determine policies, see that standards are maintained, and raise money.

SOCIAL EDUCATION AND ACTION COMMITTEES

Two of the questions in the field of health that are of greatest concern to the social education and action committees of the churches in Canada and the United States are: first, the high cost of health; and second, the quality of the treatment of mental illness.

The high cost of health. Medical costs are soaring on both sides of the border. The Methodist Church reports that the average cost per day in its hospitals rose from $20.33 in 1955 to $28.82 in 1960. A study of Canadian families revealed that the average wage-earners cannot afford to meet the overwhelming expenses that result from a severe accident, a serious disease, or a long illness.

Who should bear the costs of medical care? The General Synod of the Anglican Church of Canada has stated its conviction that: ". . . the highest attainable standard of health is one of the fundamental rights of all human beings and should be a primary care and responsibility of the nation."

Many church members do not agree with this position or with that taken by the General Board of the National Council of Churches, U.S.A., in its 1960 Pronouncement on The Churches' Concern for Health Services:

The churches' concept of man . . . imposes a more fundamental obligation for the furtherance of health. Therefore, the availability and financing of medical care of high quality is of deep concern to the churches. . . . If voluntary prepayment plans cannot accomplish the desired ends, government should protect the health of the people by making possible the prepayment of health servies.

Treatment of mental illness. Church leaders are concerned about the inadequate treatment that is being given in cases of mental illness. They are studying the problem and calling it to the attention of church members and of others who can help to remedy the situation.

EVALUATION OF THE HEALING MINISTRY OF THE CHURCHES

Churches were among the early pioneers in the building of hospitals and other agencies of healing. They were responsible for building the first hospitals in many communities. Church-related hospitals today are carrying a significant share of the load in the maintenance of general hospitals, but they are doing very little toward the treatment of tuberculosis, other chronic diseases, and mental illness. The connection between the churches and their healing institutions is weaker than that with any other of their social agencies, and church members carry only a small fraction of the cost of their maintenance.

Church leaders acknowledge their share of responsibility for the chasm that has separated the medical and religious communities, and they rejoice in the fact that bridges of understanding are being built between physicians and ministers. They know that only those persons who receive the benefits of both medicine and religion can be made whole, and they are glad that physicians and ministers are coming to understand and appreciate the contributions made by each group.

Church leaders rejoice in the tremendous strides that are being made in the healing arts, but they are deeply concerned about the rising cost of medical care. Many profound questions are yet to be answered concerning the role that churches should play in the ministry of healing in the years ahead. Among them are: Should the churches help to build the four to five thousand new hospitals that will be needed? Does the church make its best witness through the owning and operating of hospitals and other agencies or can it perform its Christian service in those that are maintained by other agencies? What are the essentially Christian factors in the healing process? Who should pay the bills for medical costs? Is first class service to be denied to persons who cannot afford to pay for it? These and other questions will engage the minds and hearts of Christian leaders in the decade ahead.

CHAPTER SIX

Disturbed Persons

Teach me to feel another's woe,
    To hide the fault I see;
That mercy I to others show,
    That mercy show to me.
        —Alexander Pope, in "The Universal Prayer"

Three groups of persons who are deeply disturbed and
who carry heavier burdens than they can manage alone
are unmarried mothers, alcoholics, and narcotics addicts.
Let us consider the problems that each of these groups
faces and see what Christians are doing to help them.

UNMARRIED MOTHERS

Each year about two hundred thousand babies are born
to unmarried mothers in the United States. About 40 per
cent of the mothers are young girls in their teens. Who are
these girls? Colonel Jane E. Wrieden says that all sorts of
women and girls come to The Salvation Army homes and
hospitals to have their babies: persons from all races and
from all national and religious groups. Some are teen-age
girls, others women in their thirties and forties; some have

had limited education, while others are college graduates; some are domestic workers, and others are professional women.

Protestant agencies provide a variety of services for the young women whose babies are to be born out of wedlock. Among these are: counseling, institutional care during pregnancy and delivery, care in foster homes, and placement of the child, if the parents desire it. Let us see what churches are doing in each of these types of service.

Counseling. Most of the girls who give birth to children out of wedlock are disturbed, unhappy persons who are seeking love and emotional security. The realization that she is to have a child outside of marriage can be a severe emotional shock to an unstable girl. She is in desperate need of wise counsel and a helping hand. She needs the assurance, found in the Christian faith, that sin can be forgiven and that she and her child can find places of dignity and worth in the world. Many church agencies and institutions employ Christian caseworkers who help girls during this time of crisis.

THE PROTESTANT EPISCOPAL CHURCH maintains seventeen regional agencies that give counsel to unwed mothers and offer casework service to the disturbed persons who are referred to them. These agencies, which were begun early in the twentieth century, are still known in some cities as the Church Mission of Help, but most of them identify themselves by the more modern name of Youth Consultation Service.

LUTHERAN AGENCIES counsel a large number of unwed mothers each year. Twenty Lutheran agencies reported that in 1960 they gave counsel to 2,047 unmarried mothers. More than one third of these women (732) awaited the birth of the children in their own homes, while the others lived in foster homes or in maternity homes.

Institutional care. Several denominations maintain homes for unmarried mothers; among them are the Protestant Episcopal Church with four homes, The Methodist Church with two, and the United Church of Christ with one. The Salvation Army maintains thirty-six maternity homes and hospitals; most of them are in cities where girls can come from the surrounding communities. The work done at Woodhaven is representative of the others:

WOODHAVEN, Fort Wayne, Indiana, is operated by the United Church of Christ. It is designed to take care of sixteen girls. The director says:

This is not the place for just sitting out an unwanted pregnancy in a dull and stagnant environment. It is a place where a girl struggling with guilt and other emotional problems can receive skilled counseling. This is where a girl can be helped to face the future with self-confidence.

In addition to therapy, the staff gives instruction in sewing, cooking, ceramics, and art. An adoption service places the babies, if the parents decide that such action is what they want.

Care in foster homes. Some church agencies believe

that unmarried mothers can lead more normal lives in foster homes than in institutions. A girl who was on the verge of insanity as she struggled alone with her problem sought the aid of the LUTHERAN WELFARE SOCIETY OF IOWA, which placed her in a foster home. The counselor and members of the foster family helped her to find her way again, as she awaited the birth of the child. She expressed her gratitude to both counselor and family in a letter to the caseworker:

Here I am, an unwed mother, completely at ease in this family. It is a wonderful experience to be welcomed so completely. The most meaningful thing of all is to be around people who are so whole that they can put one entirely at ease. . . . I feel that I am truly on my way up again.

Placement of children. About half of the children born out of wedlock are released for adoption. THE METHODIST HOME AND HOSPITAL in New Orleans, Louisiana, cares for the mother during pregnancy and delivery and maintains a licensed adoption agency that places the child, if the mother wishes. Miss Evelyn Murphee, caseworker for the institution, indicates why many unwed mothers decide to release their babies for adoption:

These girls care enough for their babies to want for them the very best Christian home possible. By releasing their babies for adoption through a church agency they feel that each child will have a good home, two parents, and the security they want for it. They know that in this way the child will not be hurt by the mistakes they have made.

ALCOHOLICS

Alcoholism is a serious problem in both the United States and Canada. There are more than five million alcoholics in the United States and approximately 182,000 in Canada. Alcoholism in the United States is five times as prevalent as cancer (1,100,000 cases) and six times as prevalent as tuberculosis (800,000 cases). Alcoholism is a disease that can be arrested, but the process is slow and painful.

Who is an alcoholic? An alcoholic is not a person who drinks and gets drunk occasionally—or even frequently. The National Council on Alcoholism gives this description of an alcoholic:

The alcoholic suffers from an ailment which compels him to drink to drunkenness again and again, although he may be fully aware that he is damaging himself physically, hurting his family, and ruining his business, and that drinking may actually interfere with his pleasures. This compulsion is equally strong among women alcoholics.

Mrs. Marty Mann, director of the council, points out that the key word in the above statement is "compels"—that the alcoholic has lost the power of choice in the matter of drinking. According to this definition, a heavy drinker is not an alcoholic if he can stop drinking when he desires to do so. He may become one soon, but is not one yet.

Many people think that alcoholics are "bums," who live on the Skid Rows of our cities. Perhaps 5 per cent of them are in this category, but 95 per cent are scattered throughout North American society. Some of them are poor and some are rich; some are brilliant and some are stupid; some are sensitive and some are dull; some are successful in business and some are failures. About 30 per cent of all alcoholics are women. It is estimated that 85 per cent of all alcoholics are between the ages of 35 and 55, the peak years for achievement and wage earning. Many persons are "hidden alcoholics" who are compelled to drink but who are able to hide the fact from their families and friends.

What are the causes of alcoholism?   Obviously, an individual cannot become an alcoholic unless he partakes of alcoholic beverages, but only a limited number of social drinkers become alcoholics. Why is it that one person becomes an alcoholic, while another, who drinks just as often, does not?

A great deal more research will have to be done before an authoritative answer can be given to this question. While scientists are not ready to state the exact causes of alcoholism, there are indications that these are both psychological and physical. People may begin to drink for a number of psychological reasons: because others are doing so and they want to "belong," because they feel low and need a lift, because they face a situation for which they feel inadequate. If alcohol seems to help one solve today's problems, it may be used in more situations and increasing amounts tomorrow. Many persons become heavy drinkers, but not all of them become alcoholics. It is possible that alcohol affects the body chemistry of some persons in such a way that each drink triggers the need for another. In such a case, the drinker is virtually compelled to follow each drink with another until he is drunk to the point of insensibility.

Alcoholism can be arrested. For centuries little attempt was made to arrest alcoholism, but in recent years physicians and others are finding ways to help people rid themselves of this affliction. Experts say that the alcoholic must really want to stop drinking and that he must never touch liquor again. He must regard it as the poison that it has become for him. If feelings of inadequacy have led the alcoholic to begin drinking, he will need psychological counseling to help him solve his problems in a more constructive way.

Three agencies have been particularly helpful in arresting alcoholism and have served as resources to church groups as they work on this problem. They are Alcoholics Anonymous, the Yale University Center of Alcohol Studies, and the National Council on Alcoholism. Brief descriptions of the contributions made by each agency follow:

ALCOHOLICS ANONYMOUS began in 1935 when two alcoholics decided to help each other stay sober "for one more day." Although A.A. keeps no records, it is estimated that this fellowship has helped three hundred thousand persons in Canada and the United States to rid themselves of alcoholism. The Preamble to the A.A. Constitution states the organization's purpose as follows:

Alcoholics Anonymous is a fellowship of men and women who share their experience, strength, and hope with each other that they may solve their common problem and help others to recover from alcoholism.

The only requirement for membership is the desire to stop drinking. There are no fees or dues for A.A. membership; we are self-supporting through our own contributions. A.A. is not allied with any sect, denomination, politics, organization, or institution; does not wish to engage in any controversy, neither endorses nor opposes any causes. Our primary purpose is to stay sober and help other alcoholics achieve sobriety.

John Park Lee, secretary of Health and Welfare, Board of National Missions of the United Presbyterian Church, U.S.A., says that Alcoholics Anonymous is successful because it meets five basic needs of an alcoholic: it gives him hope that he can recover, since he sees others who have done so; it receives him back into the human race after many doors have been closed to him; it helps him to accept his alcoholism and to understand it; it helps him to accept himself as a human being who has strengths and weaknesses as others have; and finally, it helps him to enter into relationship with God.

While A.A. is not affiliated with any religious group, it does believe that alcoholics must rely on a higher power, or "God as we understand him." While reliance on God is difficult for alcoholics who have been hostile to him, many of them do come to a deep, personal relationship with him.

Although A.A. wishes to remain anonymous, ministers and others can find out where the group meets in their communities by writing Alcoholics Anonymous, P. O. Box 459, Grand Central Station, New York 17, New York.

THE YALE UNIVERSITY CENTER OF ALCOHOL STUDIES, which in 1961 left Yale to become the RUTGERS CENTER OF ALCOHOL STUDIES, is a research and educational unit that works in such fields as psychology, biochemistry, sociology, economics, anthropology, political science, history, and documentation; and in such applied fields as medicine, religion, education, and social work. Researchers speak of the *alcoholisms*, rather than of alcoholism, since one of the center's major points of recent years is that there is not just one thing called alcoholism and that this false perception is itself a major barrier to control or prevention of any of the alcoholisms. Even consideration of the alcoholisms seems to them too narrow a view of the total area of investigation. They are concerned also with such problems as driving while under the influence of alcohol, accidents and absenteeism related to alcohol use, problems of youth and alcohol, the Skid Row derelicts, relevant problems of government (legislation, adjudication, administration, enforcement, penalization), alcohol problems and minority groups, conflict about alcohol in politics, in education, in and among religious groups, and many more.

For seven years, beginning in 1944, this group sponsored the Yale Plan Clinics, in which an alcoholic could have his problem diagnosed by an internist and a psychiatrist for the purpose of recommending treatment. He might be sent to a private physician, a hospital, or another agency. He was encouraged to develop interests, associations, and habits that would take the place of drinking. Although the Yale Plan Clinics have now been discontinued, about two hundred similar clinics have been opened in the United States and Canada, most of them modeled directly or indirectly on the Yale units.

The Center of Alcohol Studies now devotes itself entirely to research, research training, and research communication. Its objective research has tremendous value for action groups. This is recognized by the large numbers of clergymen who have attended the annual Yale University Summer School of Alcohol Studies. They average about 23 per cent of the total student body.

NATIONAL COUNCIL ON ALCOHOLISM, 2 East 103rd Street, New York 29, New York. The council takes no position on whether or not non-alcoholics should drink, but devotes all its energy to helping alcoholics refrain from doing so. Its primary function is to serve as a clearinghouse for information about alcoholism and how to arrest it; it also assists local communities in establishing information centers.

Churches assist persons who are alcoholics. Probably the greatest single contribution that churches make to alcoholics and their families is the counsel that ministers give them. The moralistic attitude of some ministers may make their counsel of little value. However, an increasing number of them have prepared themselves for giving valuable assistance by attending summer schools for alcohol studies. Several denominations hold workshops for clergymen to help them become more skilled in counseling alcoholics and their families.

Many ministers have been greatly helped by a book written by a Methodist minister: *Understanding and Counseling the Alcoholic; Through Religion and Psychology,* by Howard J. Clinebell, Jr.[1] This profound and practical book brings together insights from four dynamic sources: the Christian faith as interpreted by theologians such as Paul Tillich; psychology as taught by the William A. White Institute of Psychiatry; the scientific approach of the Yale University Center of Alcohol Studies; and the practical, redemptive experience provided by Alcoholics Anonymous.

Many churches offer their facilities as meeting places for Alcoholics Anonymous. Church members often take the lead in establishing treatment centers in their communities. The Salvation Army and several denominations operate rescue missions in the slum areas of many cities, which help some alcoholics to begin again. The Episcopal Diocese of California maintains the Henry Ohlhoff House in San Francisco as a hospice for male alcoholics seeking rehabilitation. Some of the hospitals and other welfare agencies of the church maintain staff members whose chief work is with alcoholics. For example, Chap-

[1] Nashville: Abingdon Press, 1956.

lain John Keller of the Lutheran Welfare Society of Minnesota gives full time to counseling with them.

A number of local congregations of the Church of the
Brethren help alcoholics to reestablish themselves in the
community after they have completed treatment for alcoholism. A man may live in the home of one of the church
members and be given a job in a business enterprise conducted by another; he also participates in the life of the
congregation. When he has gained sufficient security
through association within these Christian fellowships, he
is able to return to his own home town.

Churches study the alcohol question. The most comprehensive denominational program of education about alcoholism is probably that conducted by the General Board
of Temperance of The Methodist Church (100 Maryland
Ave, N.E., Washington 2, D. C.) It publishes books and
pamphlets on both temperance and the treatment of alcoholism and has prepared a very helpful "Pastor's Packet
on Alcoholism."

The United Church of Canada appointed a Commission
on Temperance Policy and Program that made a comprehensive report to the General Council in 1960. The report was adopted and is available in pamphlet form.

The International Convention of the Disciples of Christ
recommended that every church undertake a program of
alcohol education that would reach the whole congregation and its membership groups.

The proportion of drinkers in the population. According

to the Gallup Poll there has been a downward trend in the proportion of drinkers to abstainers among adults in the United States; but in Canada the proportion of drinkers is rising. The following table indicates the downward trend in the United States: [1]

Year	Drinkers	Abstainers
1945	67%	33%
1946	67%	33%
1947	63%	37%
1949	58%	42%
1950	60%	40%
1951	59%	41%
1952	60%	40%
1956	60%	40%
1957	58%	42%
1958	55%	45%
1960	62%	38%

The United Church of Canada reports that in 1943, 59 per cent of all Canadians over fifteen years of age used alcoholic beverages, but that by 1955 the proportion of those who used them had increased to 72 per cent.

NARCOTICS ADDICTS

A narcotics addict is one who has become so dependent on addicting drugs that he is under compulsion to use them continually. This compulsion is both psychological and

[1] Burgess, Roger. *Drinking Problems*, p. 4. Washington, D.C.: Division of Temperance and General Welfare, General Board of Christian Social Concerns, The Methodist Church, 1961.

physical. The need that drives an individual to the regular use of narcotics is usually a severe emotional problem from which he is trying to escape. A relatively few persons become addicts through the prolonged medical use of narcotics to relieve pain during illness. Whatever the reason for the establishment of the habit, once the body has become accustomed to the drug it is a physical necessity, and the user is "hooked." Any attempt to stop using the drug results in excruciating pain and nausea.

The Federal Bureau of Narcotics estimated that there were more than 45,000 active addicts in the United States on January 1, 1960. Other authorities believe this figure to be too conservative. The fact that possessing narcotic drugs is a crime punishable by law (except for persons permitted to handle them for medical purposes) means that users must be secretive about their addiction; therefore no completely authoritative figure is possible. Addiction is highest in large urban centers, with New York City and San Francisco in the forefront as centers of the narcotics traffic.

The cost of addiction. The relatively small number of narcotics addicts, compared to the figures for those who are alcoholics, may make this seem a minor problem in the national structure, but nothing could be more deceptive than to believe that the problem affects only those who are addicted or who are likely to become addicted. Other thousands of persons become victims of the narcotics traffic through the crime that addiction breeds.

An investigating committee of the United States Congress determined several years ago that one fourth of all the nation's crime was directly traceable to the traffic in narcotics. There is little reason to believe that this figure has changed substantially. The narcotics addict, however law-abiding and amiable his natural temperament, is almost inevitably driven to crime by his need for drugs. The cost of heroin and the other addicting drugs is so high that only a wealthy person can pay for them out of his normal income. An addict may need up to seven shots a day, with the cost varying from $20 to $50; multiply by seven and the tab becomes from $140 to $350 a week.

Robbery in all its forms, sometimes involving violence, and "pushing"—selling drugs to others—supports the habit of most male addicts. Women usually resort to shoplifting or prostitution, or both. Crime becomes a way of life.

This fact becomes more alarming when we learn that over half the known addicts in the United States are between the ages of twenty-one and thirty. During the early adult years when an individual's relationship to society is apt to harden into a mold, these young people are driven to lawlessness and degeneracy.

Drug addiction can be arrested. The addict who wishes to withdraw from narcotics faces a gruelling experience. The pain and illness involved in physical withdrawal are so severe that medical help is necessary during the process. The person who gets through the rigors of withdrawal and believes himself cured then faces his second—and more difficult problem—rehabilitation. He must, somehow, rid himself of the emotional conflicts that led him to addiction, or sooner or later he will resort to it again. Psychiatric counseling is indicated.

The Public Health Service of the United States maintains two treatment centers, one in Lexington, Kentucky, and one in Fort Worth, Texas, that offer medical care during withdrawal and psychological counseling. However, their combined capacity is less that 2,500. The number of state, city, and private hospitals that offer reasonably adequate care for addicts is negligible. In general, they give help only during physical withdrawal and release the patient to return to his old haunts, his old problems, and almost inevitably to his addiction.

In Canada, the provincial governments of British Columbia and Ontario maintain treatment centers in connection with penal institutions. However, as in the United States, the available facilities fall short of need.

Under these circumstances, can an addict—does an addict ever—recover from his affliction? The answer is that it can and does happen, though rarely. The fact that it is possible to arrest narcotics addiction means that we need more and better facilities for addicts, in order that adequate help can be offered to all who are ready to accept it.

What are the churches doing? A few—a very few—church groups are helping addicts and ex-addicts. This aid is in the form of direct help to the affected individual and his family and indirect help by means of influencing legislation. The following examples are representative of church action in this field:

THE EAST HARLEM PROTESTANT PARISH in New York City maintains a Narcotics Center under the direction of the Rev. Norman C. Eddy. The work of the center includes meetings of addicts, ex-addicts, their families and friends, at which an attempt is made to get at the roots of problems. Addicts are urged to enter one of the treatment centers in New York or in Lexington, Kentucky. Where this is not possible, a doctor who gives his services to the Narcotics Center supplies medication to help those who want to make the effort to withdraw at home. Special care is given to persons who have completed withdrawal. They are helped to find jobs and to solve family problems that may have contributed to their addiction. Particular attention is given to recreation to help relieve the terrible loneliness of the ex-addict who fears that association with his former friends will eventually lead him again to the use of drugs.

Brigadier Dorothy Berry of the Salvation Army Counsels many addicts and ex-addicts about hospital placement, job-hunting, and lodging. She is a counselor for the members of Narcotics Anonymous, an organization similar to Alcoholics Anonymous in the services it provides to addicts.

JUDSON MEMORIAL CHURCH in Greenwich Village, New York, attempts to minister to the narcotics problem by developing and discovering new techniques of working with narcotics addicts. This experimentation in the form of the Village Aid and Service Center seeks to spell out the church's role in developing a needed community service. Providing the locale for informal contacts and a professional counseling service, this neighborhood center provides an openness to this great problem in the community. The service includes psychotherapy, vocational counseling and training, pastoral counseling, and education. It seeks to help men and women develop constructive working relationships and reconstruct their personal lives.

Legislation. It was Bishop Charles H. Brent of the Protestant Episcopal Church who first worked for international control of the traffic in narcotics, after he had seen the ravages caused by addiction in the Philippine Islands. He wrote to President Theodore Roosevelt suggesting a world conference that he hoped would establish such controls. A number of conferences grew out of his proposal, and today two agencies of the United Nations are responsible for the control of narcotic drugs: The Permanent Central Opium Board, which attempts to determine the legitimate needs of each country for opium and its derivatives; and the Commission on Narcotic Drugs, which tries to enforce international agreements that would prevent the importation into any country of more narcotics than are needed for medical purposes. However, growers of the narcotics-producing plants still find ways to channel their surplus crops into illicit channels.

Concerned church leaders in the United States are working for legislation that would allow a more realistic—and a more humane—approach to the problem of narcotics addiction. The narcotics addict must be recognized as a sick person rather than a criminal, and in some way adequate treatment, rather than imprisonment, should be provided for him.

THE ANGLICAN CHURCH OF CANADA has given considerable thought to the problem of narcotics addiction. After several years of study, a Special Committee on Narcotics Addiction reported to the Executive Council of the General Synod in September, 1960. The council accepted the report of the special committee and expressed its convictions in these resolutions:

BE IT RESOLVED

That this Council gives general approval to the view expressed in the Report of the General Synod Committee to the effect that, in the light of available knowledge, the most effective way of treating the narcotics addict and of preventing further traffic is by the establishment of treatment centers under the joint auspices of the Federal and provincial governments, such centers to be in the nature of psychiatric hospitals situated within security walls, with provision for voluntary and compulsory treatment and a controlled rehabilitation and gradual reintroduction into the community.

That the Federal government be requested to take the initiative in exploring with the provinces concerned the establishment without delay of special, separate hospitals as appropriate facilities for the treatment of narcotics addicts.

EVALUATION OF WORK WITH
DISTURBED PERSONS

The loving, redemptive, healing ministry of the churches reaches out to many unmarried mothers and alcoholics to help them find themselves. It offers them assurance and security in the fellowship of the Christian community. On the other hand, most church leaders know very little about narcotics addiction. Those ministers who are concerned about the persons suffering from it are giving valiant leadership in the field.

Church members should become better informed about the causes of alcoholism and of narcotics addiction and be more helpful in their prevention. They also need to learn how to be more helpful in the rehabilitation of alcoholics and narcotics addicts.

So far, the churches have not built institutions for the rehabilitation of alcoholics and narcotics addicts, as they have done for the physically and mentally ill and the handicapped. It may not be necessary for them to do so; however, church leaders should take a more active part in determining how private and government agencies can be more helpful in the rehabilitation of these children of God.

CHAPTER SEVEN

Economic Dependents

> If a brother or sister is ill-clad and in lack of daily
> food, and one of you says to them, "Go in peace, be
> warmed and filled," without giving them the things
> needed for the body, what does it profit? James 2.15,
> 16.

Since the beginning of the Christian church, when the
apostles collected money for the poor, Christians have felt
responsible for helping to provide the essentials of life for
those who are in need. Our standards in regard to what
constitute the essentials have changed greatly during the
centuries, and so have the methods that churches use to
see that no one lacks them.

Very few people are starving in the United States or
Canada today, but a large number lack some of the necessities of life. Several studies of prices have indicated that it
takes between $5,000 and $6,000 for a family of four to
live in "health and decency" in the United States today.
In 1958, about three and a half million multiple-person
families, or 8 per cent of all families in the United States,
had annual incomes of less than $2,000; and nearly 12

million families, or 25 per cent of them, received less than $4,000. About 10 million unattached individuals, or three fifths of all persons living alone, received annual incomes below $3,000; two fifths received incomes below $2,000 and one fifth below $1,000. These figures, which include not only cash income but the money value of food grown and consumed, indicate that a large number of Americans cannot maintain the standard of living that is essential for health.

Who are the persons who receive these low incomes? Many of them are the aged who live on the benefits from Social Security and from other pension plans. Some of them are physically or mentally handicapped persons. Many of them are farmers and farm laborers; others are persons who have been unemployed for many weeks or months.

HOW CHURCHES HELP ECONOMIC DEPENDENTS TODAY

Many churches maintain small funds that are given or loaned to members who are in need of financial help. These funds are usually disbursed at the discretion of the minister. Churches, however, neither collect nor distribute the money that maintains those who are in most desperate need; these funds come from private and government welfare agencies.

The chief ways in which churches assist the needy are: first, through their influence upon public opinion, which helps to determine the policies of public and private welfare agencies; second, through the service of members on the boards and committees of family welfare agencies; third, through the maintenance of sheltered workshops; and fourth, through the programs of several special religious agencies, including the Volunteers of America, the Salvation Army, and Goodwill Industries.

Influence upon public opinion. Churches were once the chief molders of public opinion in Canada and the United States. They now share this responsible role with the schools, newspapers, radio, television, and other agencies, but they still carry considerable weight in determining the patterns of our common life. By arousing Christians to a realization of responsibility for the economic well-being of others, the churches undoubtedly helped make possible the shorter working day, the enactment of minimum wage laws, and the legalization of collective bargaining rights for labor unions.

The agencies for social education and action in the churches play a significant part in helping church members consider public issues and come to informed conclusions about them. Since the formulation of the "Social Ideals of the Churches" by the Federal Council of Churches (now a part of the National Council of Churches) in 1908, church leaders have been concerned about economic justice. Not all church members have agreed on such problems as what hours of work, wages, pensions, and relief benefits constitute justice, but discussion has eventually led to sufficient agreement for church leaders to present their views to government agencies.

One example from Canada and one from the United States will illustrate the ways in which churches help to determine economic policies today:

The Anglican Church of Canada is concerned about the increasing number of persons who are unemployed. The report of its Council for Social Service for 1960 called the attention of the church members to nine major social issues, one of which was unemployment. The report presented figures indicating the rise in unemployment and listed six reasons for its increase in Canada: (1) new technologies make obsolete the life-time skills of workers; (2) some work is seasonal in character; (3) pools of workers are unemployed between the tapering off of one piece of work and the beginning of a new one; (4) international trade results in fluctuation of employment; (5) the vast distances of Canada mean that people can be unemployed in one area while workers are needed in another; and (6) illness keeps some laborers out of work. The Council of Social Service and the Executive Council of the General Synod met jointly and adopted resolutions on important social issues. The resolution on unemployment urged:

. . . The Federal Government, in consultation with the provinces . . . and representatives of industry and labor, to take decisive action to eradicate unemployment and to initiate such manpower policies as would make it possible for every citizen to have sufficient earned income to enable him to provide adequately for his family.

The Executive Council then directed the Council for Social Service to present its views to those persons in the government "and other bodies" who are in a position to reduce unemployment in Canada.

THE UNITED CHURCH OF CHRIST in the United States is concerned about the plight of the American farmer. Despite ever increasing yields of farm products, the average income for farmers is far below that of every other group of workers in the United States. The Council for Christian Social Action held a consultation on "The Church and the Farm Problem," which called upon churchmen "to undertake a thoroughgoing study of the farm problem . . . and to play a more understanding and ethically sensitive role in the formulation of a constructive policy for American agriculture." One tool that the Council prepared to help churchmen study the farm problem was the February, 1959, issue of *Social Action*, entitled "What is Happening to the Farmer?"

Service of church members to welfare agencies. Many church members serve on the boards and committees of private welfare agencies; some of them serve on the advisory councils of the welfare agencies of the government. These persons help to determine the policies of the agencies. They listen to the convictions expressed by churchmen and other citizens and then decide what shall be the minimum standard of living that the community will help all families maintain, regardless of their ability to earn. This standard once required only cast-off clothing and small rations of food. It now includes money to buy food, clothing, shelter, and medical care for the family and schooling for the children. We still do not provide dependent families with the $4,000 to $6,000 per year that authorities agree they need for "health and decency," but the standard is rising.

Sheltered workshops. Many persons are unable to hold jobs in the competitive world of modern industry, due to physical or mental injuries, alcoholism, old age, or other disabling factors. These persons, however, are able to work in a sheltered workshop, where the foreman takes into consideration the limitations of the workers and gives them responsibilities that they can fulfill. Several church groups and church-related agencies have developed sheltered workshops where the abilities of the disabled are used. Let us look at the program of one such workshop.

GOOD SHEPHERD HOME WORKSHOP is affiliated with the Good Shepherd Home for Crippled Children and Old People in Allentown, Pennsylvania. It employs workers whose physical handicaps are so severe that they cannot find employment in industry. The manager, Bernard L. Gilbert, solicits work from industrial firms in the community; he analyzes each new job to see what physical capacities are needed to perform the task; he then matches the tasks to the abilities of workers whom private industry has classified as "disabled." These workers have made electric appliance parts, industrial metal fixtures, precision electronic items, and shoe building tools. They are paid regular wages and live in their own homes, but they eat a hot lunch at the workshop.

Special agency programs. The VOLUNTEERS OF AMERICA also operate sheltered workshops, but they work with those men who have drifted to the Skid Rows of the United States. Major J. Ford, national secretary, describes the men who are served:

America always has had a hard core of unattached men with nomadic leanings. There are perhaps a half million of them in the U.S.A. Their minimum wants are met by short-term jobs or by begging and petty pilfering. They gravitate to Skid Row for the small amount of sociability it offers and to find employment. This is the recruitment center for railroad track labor, temporary dock work, bill passers, dishwashers, offal shovelers—all menial work which steady employees prefer not to do. These men are not opposed to work, but seem incapable of sustained effort over a period of time, except under sheltered and disciplined circumstances. The average man is nearing fifty, has been married, usually at an early age, and is divorced or separated from his family.

The Volunteers provide a home for these men, a balanced diet, clothing, work in the workshop and a program of recreation and spiritual development. Many men live in these homes for a period and then are able to assume the responsibilities of normal living. Major Ford introduces us to two men who have participated in the program of the Volunteers of America:

Kenneth was the son of a county sheriff; he married young and was set up in a service station of his own by his relatives. He enlisted in World War II and served with honor, although he leaned too heavily on alcohol. When he returned home he suspected his wife of infidelity and in a rage broke up all the household furniture. He left his wife and the community and took up drinking seriously. He entered the program of the Volunteers of America and participated in group discussions on alcoholism. He remained sober for fourteen months and was given a supervisory position in the program. He was then trained in cost accounting, and a good job was obtained for him in private employment. He lasted three weeks and after a prolonged drinking bout, returned to the Volunteers' work program. He remained sober for two years and another job was obtained for him on the outside; but it lasted only till pay day. Kenneth is still with the Volunteers, is sober, and holds a respected position. He does very well in a sheltered environment, but seems totally inadequate on his own.

Max married young and was soon the father of a daughter and a son. He drove a delivery truck for a department store and managed to support his family very well for a time, but then he started to drink. He lost his job and left home. For fourteen years he divided his time between the county workhouse and the Skid Row of his own community, but did not see his wife or children during that time. He entered the program of the Volunteers of America, participated in group discussion of alcoholism, and remained sober. The first Christmas after his admission he sent presents to his wife and children. The following spring he was invited by his wife to attend the graduation of his son. Some time later he was invited to the wedding of his daughter and to a going-away party for his son, who was entering the armed forces. During his absence, his wife had made good in her job and had purchased a house and a car. Shortly after the departure of both children, the husband and wife were reunited and are still together. Man is active in A.A. and seems to have no trouble in assuming normal living, now that he has no responsibility for the children.

THE SALVATION ARMY. The Salvation Army operates homes in the slum areas of many cities. Homeless men come to them for shelter, food, and a chance to begin again. The Salvation Army supplements the services given by government agencies and assists some families and individuals who are legally disqualified for government assistance.

GOODWILL INDUSTRIES OF AMERICA. The present work of Goodwill Industries is the outgrowth of the solution a young Methodist minister in Boston found for the problems of some of his parishioners in 1902. Dr. Edgar J. Helms decided that the handicapped and unfortunate citizens of the South End of Boston needed "not charity, but a chance." Clothing and household articles were collected from housewives; handicapped men and women were taught to repair the articles, which were then sold at low cost to needy persons.

The idea spread to other cities, and the name, "Goodwill Industries," was originated by a newly formed branch in Brooklyn in 1915. The Board of Home Missions of The

Methodist Church began to support the work in 1919 and has assisted in the development of many more branches.

There are now 123 local Goodwill Industries in the United States, 8 in Canada, one in Mexico, and several in other nations. Each unit is locally autonomous, but is related to the national organization.

In 1959, more than 38,000 persons earned their living through Goodwill Industries. The disabilities of the persons employed each year tend to be in these categories: orthopedic and general handicaps, 41 per cent; mental, emotional, and social handicaps, 16 per cent; age and infirmity, 16 per cent; blind, deaf, or handicapped by speech defects, 12 per cent. The remaining 15 per cent are not handicapped, but are persons in supervisory positions.

The total income of all Goodwill Industries in 1959 was about $36,000,000. Ninety-one per cent of the income was earned by the handicapped, but support came to sixty-two local Goodwill Industries from Community Chests. The Board of Missions of The Methodist Church continues to give about $5,000 annually; all of this money is used for the training of leaders and the development of new branches.

Let us meet a man and a woman who have found new life through the Goodwill Industries:

Bernard was a bachelor. He suffered from acute arthritis and became more and more depressed as he entered old age. He was contemplating suicide when he read of the program of Goodwill Industries for elderly, handicapped persons. When he visited Goodwill's office, he was received warmly. When the personnel director discovered that Bernard had been a housepainter, she told him that they needed his help in painting furniture. Bernard has worked at Goodwill Industries for two years; he is a good worker who is always on the job. Even his arthritis seems better now.

Helen has had only 10 per cent vision all her life. She attended the Florida School for the Blind in Jacksonville and was graduated from its high school. For a time, Helen operated a vending stand maintained by the Florida Council for the Blind, but felt that she might use more of her abilities with Goodwill Industries. She soon became an inspector of garments made by others. Her fingers fly over the garments as she okays them for sale. Her forelady believes that she is more efficient than others with perfect vision. Helen's husband works in a furniture store; their combined earnings provide a comfortable living for them.

EVALUATION OF THE CHURCHES' WORK
WITH ECONOMIC DEPENDENTS

There will always be adults who need help in providing for their financial needs. Many persons who have physical and mental handicaps can be trained to hold jobs in private industry; others will be able to provide for most of their own needs through sheltered workshops and other programs. Many of the aged will be able to live on the benefits of Social Security and private pension plans, but financial assistance will be necessary for some elderly persons and others who are unable to work and whose incomes are inadequate.

Economic Dependents

Churches will want to continue to give some financial assistance to adults, at the discretion of their pastors or social workers. They will want to continue to support agencies that help adults get a new start in life or provide for their own needs under sheltered conditions, such as the Salvation Army, Goodwill Industries, Inc., and Volunteers of America.

One of the major responsibilities that Christians have for adults who are unable to provide for their own economic needs is to determine the policies that regulate their care. Church members play a large part in deciding how the needs of these persons are to be met: they influence public opinion; they serve on policy-making boards; they speak through church bodies to government officials.

Christians need to give careful consideration to the standard of living that society maintains for economically dependent adults. Should they be given only enough money for subsistence or should they be maintained in comfort? What is the standard of living that should be provided for those who cannot care for themselves? Should they have comfortable homes, palatable and healthful food, attractive clothing, dental and medical care, and some facilities for recreation?

When church members have answered these questions they will want to use their influence with the government and with private welfare agencies to see that adequate help is given, so that these children of God can live more nearly as he intends for them to live.

CHAPTER EIGHT

Migrants

The lowest group in the American social order . .
are the migratory workers. They are the lowest paid,
the most insecure, the most poorly housed, the most
socially declassed, and the most ignored.—Senator
Paul H Douglas

Tally McNeil lives in a dingy, one-room shack on the Eastern
Shore with his pregnant wife, five children, and his worries.
They share three cots, a two-burner stove, and a gnawing un-
certainty over where the next dollar will come from. "In the
last two days I ain't picked more than $2 worth of tomatoes.
. . . That don't buy us much." . . . Tally McNeil, his family, his parents, and five brothers and sisters are among the
more than five thousand migrants who swarm into Maryland
each summer to pick the crops and haul them to market. Picking beans, tomatoes, carrots, potatoes, blueberries is stoop
labor. As William McNeil explains: "You crawl along on
your knees. . . . When they begin to hurt you stand up and
pick. When your back starts bothering you, down on your
knees again."[1]

[1] Stern, Lawrence. *Maryland's Migratory Workers*, pp. 1-2. Washington, D.C.: U.S. Department of Labor, 1959.

THE MIGRANT AND HIS WORK

Who are the migrants? Technically, a migrant is a worker who has no fixed place of abode, but moves from place to place in order to earn his living. Although some other workers, such as seamen, may have no permanent homes and move about in the pursuit of their labors, the word "migrant" in common usage has come to mean an agricultural worker who moves from place to place with his family, in order to harvest the crops as they ripen.

Migrants perform essential services. Agriculture is becoming increasingly mechanized; many tasks that formerly were done by hand are now done by machine. However, many crops still must be picked by hand. When tomatoes or strawberries or blueberries ripen, the grower is in urgent need of pickers. If they do not arrive at the exact time he needs them, all his efforts will be lost. This means that the growers are dependent on migratory farm laborers.

Migrants are employed in the harvesting and processing of cotton and many fruits and vegetables. Among the fruits that are picked by hand are strawberries, blueberries, cranberries, blackberries, melons, apples, apricots, peaches, pears, oranges, and other citrus fruits. Most vegetables are hand-picked: beans, lettuce, celery, tomatoes, and sugar beets. Three fourths of the cotton is picked by hand.

Can harvesting be mechanized? Possibly the harvesting of wheat is the most mechanized of all farm processes —ten or fifteen men do in a day what formerly took twice as many men two or three weeks to do. The big combines move across the fields cutting the grain, threshing it, scattering the chaff and stalks over the land for mulch, and pouring the grain into wagons to be hauled to the elevators —all in one continuous operation.

Similar machines are in operation for the harvesting of cotton. In 1955, cotton-picking machines harvested 23 per cent of the total crop in the United States, but an abundance of cheap labor has limited their use. This fact is illustrated by the use made of these machines in different parts of the country. In California and Arizona where labor is both scarce and expensive (economists would say expensive because scarce) cotton-picking machines were used to harvest 66 and 47 per cent of the crop, respectively. In the delta states, the machines harvested 25 to 40 per cent of the crop; but in the southeastern states, where labor is plentiful and cheap, they harvested less than 3 per cent of it. As one Southern planter said, "As long as I can get cotton pickers at $3 a hundred pounds, I let my machines lie idle."[1]

Machines have been invented for picking many of the crops now harvested by hand, but they are not widely used because they are expensive to operate or spoil part of the crop in the process. No doubt machines will be invented that will greatly reduce the number of persons who are needed for hand labor in the fields.

[1] Shotwell, Louisa Rossiter. *This Is the Migrant,* p. 21. New York: Friendship Press, 1958.

Migrants move in streams. The migrant streams absorb many workers who have few skills and who have been uprooted from settled employment. Many of them are native-born, but some are foreigners. Others are imported, under contract, for the season.

Migrants tend to move in rather clearly defined streams up and down America. Contrary to the rivers, these streams tend to flow from south to north; like the rivers, very few of the migrant streams flow east and west. There are six of these streams, and quite different peoples are caught up in their movements. Herbert Hill describes the streams in these words:

Migrants, most of whom are Negroes, who start in Florida and move north along the Atlantic Seaboard through Georgia, the Carolinas and Virginia into Maryland, Delaware, New Jersey, New York and Pennsylvania, working in a wide variety of harvesting and food processing operations.

Migrants, almost all of whom are Mexican-American, who start in Texas and go into the North Central and Mountain States, working mainly in the sugar beet harvest and also picking vegetables and fruits.

Migrants, most of whom are of Mexican descent, who start in Texas and go north to Montana and North Dakota, working in the wheat and small-grain harvests.

Migrants, most of whom are Mexican-Americans and Negroes, who start in Texas and then divide into two groups, with one group moving to the Mississippi Delta and the other moving westward to New Mexico, Arizona and southern California, working in cotton.

Migrants, usually whites of early American stock, who start in

Oklahoma, Arkansas and western Tennessee, and move north and west, working in fruit and tomatoes.

Migrants, of all backgrounds, who work up and down the Pacific Coast, harvesting and processing various fruits and vegetables.[1]

Some migrants are imported under contract. When all practicable sources of our own workers have been exhausted, the United States Government arranges with the Government of Mexico for the importation of Mexican laborers. In 1955, more than four hundred thousand Mexicans were brought into the country for work in twenty-four states. The Mexican Government selects the workers and the United States Government pays for the transportation from Mexico to reception centers in the United States. The employers transport the workers from the centers to their farms and back to the centers, provide sanitary housing and cooking facilities at a maximum cost of $1.75 per day, pay the prevailing wage rates, and guarantee that the laborers will have a certain amount of employment.

Similar arrangements are made for the importation of agricultural workers from Jamaica and the Bahamas. Puerto Ricans are American citizens, but they also come to the mainland for farm work under contract. Despite some of the difficulties that arise concerning "prevailing wages" and other problems, the foreign and Puerto Rican contractual

[1] *No Harvest for the Reaper,* by Herbert Hill, National Association for the Advancement of Colored People, 20 West 40th St., New York, N. Y. Used by permission.

workers have more protection than many of the migrants who were born in the United States.

THE MINISTRY TO MIGRANTS

The services that Protestant churches render to migrants are probably better co-ordinated than any of their other welfare activities. Practically all the work that is done is interdenominational in character, and most of the denominations affiliated with the National Council of Churches participate in it. Before considering the problems of the migrants and how the churches help them, let us look at the history of the ministry to migrants.

The origins of the migrant ministry. Shortly after World War I, the Interchurch World Movement of North America made a survey of the problems faced by migratory workers on the East Coast. The survey disclosed very acute problems of housing, sanitation, and morals; and recommended that church agencies train "itinerant missionaries who would follow the migratory movement itself as counselors and companions of the transient workers."

Two agencies, the Home Missions Council of North America and the Council of Women for Home Missions,[1] heard the report and decided to begin work in a center in New Jersey, one in Delaware, and two in Maryland. The work began in the summer of 1920.

The workers took care of young children while the

[1] These agencies now constitute the Division of Home Missions of the National Council of Churches.

mothers worked in the fields. The reports indicate that the children grabbed their food "like little wild things and ran for the shacks to hide their plunder." But order gradually emerged and the children learned to help prepare a hot lunch, set the table, wash the dishes, sing songs, and play games.

Other centers and workers were added. In 1922, twenty workers fed and cared for 199 children in six centers, all of which were open from dawn to dark for eleven weeks during the summer. Early in the program, college students were enrolled as staff assistants.

The first migrant missionary nurse, Eva Barnes, went to work in 1926 in California's Imperial Valley. In her battered "Chevrolita" she made regular visits to twenty-three camps. In one month she visited 1,850 homes, gave treatment or referral for 314 infections, 119 colds, 117 pregnancies, 34 cases of scabies, and 19 cases of venereal disease. Her enthusiasm was contagious. She soon enlisted a number of volunteer helpers: three physicians, a Japanese nurse, a Korean dentist, and many teachers. She supervised sixteen Sunday schools that met "with God's sunshine overhead and the cotton fields backstage." The migrants called her the "Jesus Nurse."

The depression of the 1930's set more and more migrants on the road, and it reduced the financial resources of the migrant ministry. Despite this fact, more volunteers were enlisted and the program was expanded.

Self-evaluation after forty years. In 1960, the migrant

ministry celebrated its fortieth anniversary. In preparation for this event, the National Migrant Committee of the Division of Home Missions of the National Council of Churches instituted a study of its work. Migrant committees in thirty-four states co-operated in the study by answering questionnaires and participating in eight area workshops. The findings of this study were brought together in a report entitled *The Migrant Ministry Today*. Galen R. Weaver, at that time chairman of the National Migrant Committee, indicated in the foreword how the migrant ministry has grown:

In 1920, four centers were set up to give day care to the babies of migrant fruit and vegetable workers in New Jersey, Maryland, and Delaware. In 1960, 500 employed workers and 8,000 volunteers conducted social and religious programs for migrant people of all ages in thirty-four states.[1]

The sponsorship of the program has broadened as the work has grown. The migrant ministry now enlists the active co-operation of state and local councils of churches, state and local councils of church women, and the National Council of Churches. In addition it calls upon student organizations to help enlist hundreds of college students, who spend their summer vacations in the migrant ministry.

Direct services to migrants. The migrant ministry ren-

[1] *The Migrant Ministry Today*, a self-evaluation of direct services and progress toward legislative goals, p. 3. New York: Division of Home Missions, National Council of Churches, 1960.

ders several services to migrant families: religious services, child care, special schools for children, vocational training, and adult education.

THE RELIGIOUS MINISTRY. The migrant ministry is rooted in the church and is motivated by religious convictions, yet its religious services vary greatly. The programs in most of the camps include Sunday schools and Daily Vacation Bible Schools. The workers start with the children where they are and lead them into experiences of play, work, and worship. The children are hungry for love. One worker reported that the children know that God makes the trees, the fruits, and the vegetables, but have not been able to go far beyond that. One child asked, "Does God really love me?"

Since the teachers find it difficult to use the regular church school materials, denominational leaders have cooperated in preparing Christian educational materials for use with migrant children. These materials help the children understand and cope with the problems they and their parents face.

In some states, the workers try to draw migrants into the churches in the community, but this effort is not very successful. Others hold preaching services in the camps. Sometimes the workers preach and conduct the services; at other times ministers of the same background as the migrants may be asked to speak. One worker in Colorado reports that when José helped him set up the center for a worship service, he said, "Mr. Bill, that's a funny kind of a cross. It hasn't got any body on it." When the worker explained why the Protestant cross is empty, José exclaimed, "Oh, I didn't know he was still alive!"

After a worker in a Michigan camp finished preaching a sermon at a family night program, a migrant said, "Come again, won't you? You sure bring God with you when you come."

CHILD-CARE CENTERS. In eight states the migrant ministry maintains child-care centers in the migrant camps. They take care of children while the parents are in the fields.

SPECIAL SCHOOLS. One of the great problems of the migrants is that they rarely stay long enough in one place for their children to go to school. The migrant ministry conducts special schools for these children in six states, but in others the state government provides the schools and the workers urge the children to attend them.

VOCATIONAL TRAINING. Many migrants hope that their children will be able to learn trades and settle in normal communities, but it is difficult for the children to learn any vocation except harvesting the crops. Four vocational training projects were begun in New Jersey in 1957 and have been continued since then.

After the boys returned from the fields they were taught the fundamental rules and practices of carpentry. They built two full-sized cabins, such as they may eventually make for themselves. They also learned to repair doors, screens, and windows in their own cabins.

The girls were taught homemaking: how to prepare in-expensive but well-balanced meals; how to sew (they fur-nished the cabins the boys made); and how to care for chil-dren.

It is hoped that these experimental projects can be ex-panded to other camps.

ADULT EDUCATION. The migrant ministry in ten states conducts classes to teach migrants to read and write. Spanish-speaking people are also taught English. One father of eight in a New Jersey camp was persistent—at the end of the summer he was able to read and write.

The ministry's legislative goals. For many years lead-ers of the migrant ministry have been concerned about legislation that would remedy some of the situations faced by the migrants. The National Migrant Committee drew up a set of legislative goals that it presented to the National Council of Churches. In 1951, the National Council adopted the goals and sent them to its constituent groups in the form of a pronouncement called "The Concern of the Churches for Agricultural Migratory Labor." Denomi-national bodies, state and local councils of churches, and some local churches either endorsed these goals or adopted similar ones. The goals dealt with the most difficult prob-lems of the migrants: housing, welfare, and health services; public education; child labor; imported labor; minimum wages; practices of crew leaders and labor contractors; and transportation.

The 1960 study conducted by the National Migrant

Committee (see page 147) was an attempt to see the extent to which the goals adopted in 1951 had been achieved. Some goals had been reached in Federal legislation but still needed supplementary action by state governments. Let us look at the goals stated in the pronouncement "The Concern of the Churches for Agricultural Migratory Labor" (the italicized statements below), at what has been achieved, and at what remains to be done:

HOUSING. *". . . the churches should support measures intended to provide . . . a Federal housing code for migrant camps to set a minimum standard for all states."*

A Federal housing code has not yet been adopted; but thirteen states have adopted housing and/or sanitation codes that apply to the housing of farm laborers. Even when codes are adopted, enforcement is still a problem.

WELFARE AND HEALTH SERVICES. *". . . the churches should support measures intended to provide . . . the extension to migratory farm workers and their families by the communities in which they are employed the health and welfare services available to their own residents."*

Replies from state Migrant Committees indicate that health services are available to migrants in twelve states and that partial services are available in sixteen others. Much more needs to be done to extend community services to migrants.

PUBLIC EDUCATION. *". . . the churches should support measures intended to provide . . . improved educational facilities for migratory workers and their children."*

The committees in twenty states report that it is compulsory for children under sixteen to attend school when they are in session. The committee in Florida points out that migrant children are often too retarded educationally to fit into the public schools. The Wisconsin Committee reports that the University of Wisconsin is experimenting with teaching methods that will make maximum use of the brief periods students are in school.

CHILD LABOR. *". . . the churches should support measures intended to provide . . . the protection of the children of migratory workers by more effective enforcement of the Fair Labor Standards Act as amended in 1950 to make it compulsory for children under sixteen to attend schools while schools are in session."*

Eleven state committees report that child labor laws apply to the children of migrants in their states; six committees report that regulations are enforced.

IMPORTED LABOR. *". . . the churches should support measures intended to provide . . . [for] the importation of foreign workers only when necessary to supplement the domestic labor supply, with adequate provision made for their welfare."*

Eleven committees reported that Public Law 78 (which specifies that imported labor may not be brought into an area unless domestic labor is unavailable) is enforced in their states; three others report that the law is partially enforced.

MINIMUM WAGES. *". . . the churches should support*

measures intended to provide . . . the extension of minimum wage legislation, social security benefits, and labor legislation to include migratory farm laborers."

Twenty-five committees report that they do not have a minimum wage law that is applicable to agriculture; Wisconsin alone reports a minimum wage scale.

CREW LEADERS AND LABOR CONTRACTORS. *". . . the churches should support measures to provide . . . a plan for the effective recruitment, fair employment practices, and equitable distribution of seasonal farm laborers."*

Eight state committees report that registration is required for crew leaders and labor contractors.

TRANSPORTATION. *". . . the churches should support measures intended to provide . . . the regulation of the methods of transportation of workers from area to area and from state to state to insure their humane treatment."*

The Interstate Commerce Commission was granted the authority, in 1956, to establish requirements for "certain" as distinguished from "common" carriers of migrant farm workers. The regulations apply to transportation of seventy-five miles or more across a state line. Ten state committees report supplementary state legislation, six report none, and six report partial regulation.

EVALUATION OF WORK WITH MIGRANTS

Protestant churches have made and are making a significant contribution through their ministry to migratory agricultural workers. Several important factors are combined that make this one of the outstanding social welfare programs of the churches. Among these factors are:

First, the ministry has rendered direct services to hundreds of thousands of migrant workers and their families. It has given food and clothing, medical aid, child care, and education for both children and adults; and it has also provided religious services and Christian education for them.

Second, the ministry has called attention to the essential contribution that migrants make to the American economy and to the problems that they face. It has made growers more appreciative of their services and has led them to provide better wages and conditions of work for migrants. It has made community leaders aware of these workers and has helped them to realize that migrants are entitled to share in the resources of the community, since they are temporary residents of it.

Third, the ministry has developed a wise legislative strategy. It drew up a well-balanced program for the improvement of the working and living conditions for migratory workers. It then presented the program to the General Assembly of the National Council of Churches for adoption. This procedure not only gave authority to the legislative program but secured the support of many influential leaders for it. The ministry then called upon its friends throughout the country to work for the program, and after nine years made a study to see how much of the program had been adopted and how effectively the laws were being enforced.

Fourth, the program is nationwide. Its leaders are in regular communication with one another.

Fifth, the program is interdenominational. This means that there is little duplication of effort and that the resources available for the program can be used most advantageously.

Sixth, the leaders are aware of the fact that machinery will one day do much of the work now done by migrants. The ministry is developing an educational program that will help migrants learn skills that will prepare them for other types of work.

Seventh, the ministry does not confine itself to one method of work, but combines social service with social education and action.

One of the chief problems faced by the migrant ministry is that of financial support. Its resources have always been too slender for the scope and significance of its work. In future, it will need increased resources both in money and personnel if it is to achieve the goals that have been set for it.

CHAPTER NINE

Prisoners, Parolees, and Ex-Prisoners

It is acknowledged that neither convict prisons, nor the hulks, nor any system of hard labor ever cured a criminal.—Fëdor Dostoevski

Revenge against one's enemies has frequently been a characteristic of primitive societies. If the enemy put out one of a man's eyes, he or his relatives did not rest until they had put out both of his. The ancient Jewish law of an "eye for an eye, and a tooth for a tooth" was a reform measure designed to restrict the scope of retribution. Jesus renounced even this modified law and told his followers to love their enemies and to pray for them. Instead of loving their neighbors only, they were to love their enemies also.

Jesus' admonition to love our enemies has not been followed in our treatment of prisoners. In the early centuries following Jesus' time, persons who were convicted of crimes were subjected to torture and inhuman treatment. There were no real prisons in Europe until Bridewell Prison was established in London in 1553. Prior to that time prisoners were farmed out to private persons, whose only responsibility was to keep them in custody.

THE BEGINNINGS OF MODERN PENOLOGY

The foundation of criminal science was laid in 1764 by the publication of a treatise by C. B. Beccaria entitled *On Crimes and Punishments*. Mr. Beccaria taught that the sole justification for legal punishment was the protection of society by the prevention of crime and that the cruel treatment of prisoners and capital punishment were not only wrong but ineffective. During the latter part of the eighteenth century, John Howard advocated reform principles that were not adopted but that later guided penology.

The Society of Friends and Elizabeth Fry, who worked tirelessly in Newgate Prison in the early 1800's, had considerable effect on the treatment of prisoners. While the measures they advocated were not adopted in England until a much later date, they led to the development of the Pennsylvania System of prison discipline that was to influence penology in Europe as well as North America.

The conviction that prisons should reform criminals rather than punish them developed in the late nineteenth century, particularly in the 1870's. Some attempts were made to follow this principle but little was done until the twentieth century, and much still remains to be done.

WHAT ARE CHURCHES DOING?

Churches in Canada and the United States are concerned about prisoners while they are in prison and after their release. They are helping them in three ways:

gh study, education, and action concerning the best
ods of treatment of prisoners; through the chaplaincy
e; and through programs for the rehabilitation of pris-
who are paroled or released. Let us consider each of
channels of service in more detail.

cial education and action. The committees for social
ation and action in Protestant churches are concerned
ut two major questions in relation to prisoners: the kind
treatment that will be best for the prisoners and for soci-
ty, and whether capital punishment should be abolished.

Why does society punish criminals? Is it in retribution for
the crime committed? Is it to deter others from committing
offenses? Is it to segregate persons who might commit other
crimes? Is it to reform the prisoners? All of these elements
are being discussed by Christians who are interested in finding more effective methods of treatment.

Penologists estimate that between 15 and 20 per cent of
all convicts cannot be reformed, but must be confined to
maximum-security prisons all their lives. Their release
would result in the commission of new crimes. Penologists
believe, however, that 80 to 85 per cent of the convicts can
be helped to lead law-abiding lives.

Prisons as they are now operated in the United States
and Canada do very little to help the prisoners reform. Of
the more than 175,000 prisoners who were in penal institutions in the United States in 1956, two thirds were serving
a second, third, or fourth term. About 75 per cent of Canada's prisoners are convicted of new crimes after their re-

lease. This situation is in sharp contrast to that of Great Britain, where a probation system has resulted in the rehabilitation of 75 per cent of those convicted.

Another indication of the inadequacy of the prison system of the United States is the large number of riots that occur. Between 1950 and 1956 there were nearly one hundred serious riots in the state prisons of the nation; riots occurred in most of the states. Among the defects in the prison system are overcrowding, idleness, antiquated buildings, poorly trained personnel, and interference by politicians.

Several states have experimented with new methods of treatment that are proving very successful. These new methods include psychiatric treatment, work experience that trains prisoners for trades they can follow after release, schools and correspondence courses. A few states have developed "youth authorities" that provide separate custody and expert guidance for youthful offenders. Among the states that have developed better prison systems are California, Minnesota, Wisconsin, Massachusetts, and Texas.

THE ANGLICAN CHURCH OF CANADA has given particular attention to prison reform. Its Council for Social Service has published several pamphlets on the subject and has urged members of the church to express their convictions to government authorities. A number of reforms have been instituted, among them a National Parole Board that has exclusive jurisdiction in granting, refusing, or revoking parole. Its powers extend to offenders sentenced to provincial institutions for conviction of offenses against Federal law.

Shall capital punishment be abolished? It has been abolished in many countries, particularly in Europe, Asia, and Latin America. Eight states of the United States have abolished capital punishment: Alaska, Delaware, Hawaii, Maine, Michigan, Minnesota, North Carolina, and Wisconsin. A ninth state, Rhode Island, permits it only under quite exceptional circumstances. Neither Puerto Rico nor the Virgin Islands impose the death penalty. In several other states capital punishment is sanctioned by the penal code but is not practiced. Between 1923 and 1953 the average number of executions per year in the United States was 135. About 87 per cent of these were for murder and 11 per cent for rape. The remaining 2 per cent were for armed robbery, kidnapping, burglary, and espionage.

State social education and action committees of several denominations and of councils of churches are taking an active part in the movement to abolish capital punishment. In some cases, they have been quite influential in getting this practice eliminated. What are the reasons given for and against capital punishment?

The proponents of capital punishment believe that it is necessary for three reasons: retribution, deterrence, and expense.

The basic reason why Christians oppose this practice is theological. They believe that each person is a child of God who is of infinite worth to him and that the taking of human life, which is within the providence of God, cannot be assumed by man.

Christians reject retribution as a justification for capital punishment as unworthy of a civilized nation.

Christians turn to penologists concerning the validity of the claim that capital punishment deters persons from committing crimes. What really seems to restrain them is certainty that the crime will be detected and punished.

Christians believe that cost should not be a factor in deciding an issue of life or death. However, the cost of appeals, litigation, and administration are so great that penologists have found that life imprisonment actually costs the state less than capital punishment.

Christians also believe that capital punishment should be abolished because of its brutalizing effect on police officers and on the public as a whole. There is some evidence that deranged persons are so upset by the accounts of executions that they sometimes commit murder or suicide.

One other reason given for abolishing the death penalty is the fallibility of the courts. It is not outside the range of possibility for an innocent person to be executed.

Chaplaincy service. Chaplains serve in most of the penal institutions of the country. The large Federal and state prisons may have one or more resident chaplains, while others have part-time chaplains. Chaplains are employed by most Federal and state prisons, in co-operation with national boards representing Jews, Roman Catholics, and Protestants. THE DEPARTMENT OF PASTORAL SERVICES of the National Council of Churches nominates Protestant chaplains to the Federal Bureau of Prisons. Chaplains now serving prisons come from these denominations: American Baptist, Southern Baptist, Disciples of Christ, Protestant Episcopal, Methodist, United Presbyterian, and United Church of Christ.

One example of denominational ministry to the religious needs of prisoners is the work of the PROTESTANT EPISCOPAL CHURCH. The Christian Social Relations Departments of thirty-eight dioceses surveyed the work of the chaplains in the prisons of their areas. As a result of positive findings, they are helping to sponsor chaplains in prisons where none were at work before, and they are holding in-service training sessions for all chaplains.

Assistance to parolees and ex-prisoners. Very few persons die in prison. The prisoners serve their sentences and are released. The current practice of most prisons is to give them a few clothes and a small grant of money and turn them loose. One man described the situation that released prisoners face:

We are the anonymous ones who move amongst you but not of you; constantly on guard, lest by an incautious word or gesture, we may betray ourselves to you, and thereby lose our anonymity—and your respect. You may find us in your factories, in your garages, on your farms, and, sometimes, in your offices and places of business. We live next door, work at the next lathe, sit next to you in the movies. In short, we are your neighbors. Yet we are a group set apart, divided by our experience from those around us. We are the parolees from your prisons, still doing time. Although we walk the streets to all outward appearances as free men, we wear invisible numbers.

During World War II an industrial firm received a government contract that meant every employee would have to submit to a security check. Each of the 1,600 employees was fingerprinted and the results run through the F.B.I. files. Nearly six hundred employees were found to have fingerprint records as ex-convicts. The first reaction was to fire them all, but the management decided to look at each employee's record with the firm. Most of the ex-convicts had good work records, and some of them held responsible supervisory positions. The company decided not to fire anyone, but to change its policy and cease barring ex-convicts from employment.

A few years ago, the editor of a small newspaper in the Southern part of the United States came into national prominence because one of his books became a best seller. The publicity that accompanied the book eventually brought revelation of the fact that he had served a prison sentence for a crime committed in a Northern city in his youth. There was a brief flurry of comment on this fact, several newspapers ran editorials that contrasted his long record of useful work with one youthful indiscretion, and the author went on to write more books and to become an even more popular leader. This willingness to accept and forgive a past criminal act indicates the growing maturity of the United States.

THE CHURCH: COMMUNITY OF THE REDEEMED. A number of years ago, a successful young banker was hard-pressed for cash in a business deal. He embezzled $5,000 from the bank, intending to pay it back as soon as possible. However, his act was discovered, he was found guilty and sentenced to three years in the state penitentiary.

The banker was a member of the Board of Stewards of his church. Shortly after his trial, a motion was presented to declare his post on the board vacant and to elect a successor to fill his place. One older and respected member of the board declared that this was a most unchristian procedure. He maintained that a Christian church is not a fellowship of saints who have done no wrong, but a community of the redeemed, who have committed many wrongs, but whom God has forgiven. The motion was tabled and discussion continued for many months concerning the membership of the banker on the board. As the discussion developed, the minister and the members of the board came to a wholly new concept of the meaning of forgiveness and the fact that the church is a fellowship of persons who have been forgiven for real sins.

The Board of Stewards finally voted to retain the banker as a member. The congregation was told of the decision and plans were made for the man's return to the church. On the day that he was released, the minister and the members of the board stood outside the prison gates ready to receive him. They drove back to their community and to the church, where the whole congregation took part in a communion service, which symbolized the common need of all the members to seek forgiveness.

Eventually the minister learned that the steward who

had first insisted that the banker's act be forgiven and that his membership on the board be maintained had spoken out of deep personal conviction. Many years before, as a young man, he also had stolen money from his employer; but the employer, who was a Jew, had insisted on paying the man's debt, continuing him as an employee, and arranging that he repay his debt in small installments. This act had saved his standing in the community and influenced him to lead a life of honesty—and forgiveness.

LOCAL CHURCHES HELP TO REHABILITATE EX-PRISONERS. A number of local churches help parolees and ex-prisoners to find homes and employment as soon as they are released. This work is usually done in co-operation with the chaplain of the prison, who knows the person who is to be released and can indicate the type of help he or she will need. For example, the Disciples of Christ have launched an experimental program in Indianapolis that will enlist the co-operation of several churches in the study of penal and parolee problems. Church members are being trained to counsel persons on probation or parole; their work will supplement that of parole officers and express their love as Christians.

CHURCH AGENCIES HELP TO REHABILITATE EX-PRISONERS. The experience of the Episcopal Community Service in San Diego, California, will indicate the type of work that is done by several church-related agencies.

One of the units in the Episcopal Community Service center is "The Club," which was organized in 1955 by men who were discharged from the county honor camps, located in the mountains near San Diego. The Club meets each Thursday evening at the center. After the business session, the members discuss their mutual problems and hear the stories of new men who have just been released. The chief problems of released prisoners are usually: no place to stay, no work, and no money. Members help to solve the problem of no place to stay by taking recently released prisoners into their homes for a few days, or by finding rooms for them in hotels. However, The Club plans to erect a dormitory where these men may live for the first weeks after release.

The problem of no money is solved by small loans, but the problem of no work is the most difficult. At first, members of The Club helped men find work with their own employers, but when the numbers seeking work became too great for this personal approach they decided to employ a man whose job is to serve as a full-time liaison man between The Club and prospective employers. A small-scale employment bureau was the result.

EVALUATION OF WORK WITH PRISONERS, PAROLEES, AND EX-PRISONERS

Jesus and the members of the early Christian church were far more concerned about prisoners and prison life than are church members today. One reason may be that Paul and several disciples knew about prison life from firsthand experience.

Prisoners, Parolees, and Ex-Prisoners

It is good that Christian concern for prisoners is developing along two lines: work with individuals, both while they are in prison and after their release; and consideration of the effectiveness of the penal system.

Probably the most significant work that churches are doing with prisoners is to co-operate with government authorities in providing trained clergymen to serve as prison chaplains. Each year, more chaplains are assigned to work in a greater number of prisons, and the quality of work done is steadily rising. It would be helpful if more church members had close contact with chaplains. These clergymen can help church members to learn more about our penal system; they can also increase the effectiveness of the social service work that churches do with prisoners.

Far too few church members offer any assistance to prisoners, parolees, or ex-prisoners. They do not heed the words of Jesus that he came to bring "release to captives." The direction that has been given by a few pioneering leaders should be followed by many more churches and church members.

Christians in both Canada and the United States need to give serious consideration to our prison systems. The very high percentage of prisoners who are serving second, third, fourth, and even tenth terms indicates that our penal institutions fail to reform those who are committed to them. Many Christian groups should learn the facts about our penal systems, evaluate them as Christians, and seek for methods that would redeem these children of God.

A WORD ABOUT THE FORMAT

*The text of this book is set on the Linotype in Fairfield, designed
by the distinguished American artist and engraver, Rudolph
Ruzicka. A master craftsman whose talent has long been dedicated
to clarity, he has given his type face a trim grace and virility,
coupled with a spirited design and sensitive balance.*

*Composed, printed, and bound by Book Craftsmen Associates,
Inc., New York • Jackets and paper covers printed by Affiliated
Lithographers, Inc., New York • Text paper, S. D. Warren's
No. 66 Antique Book.*

*Typographic design by Margery W. Smith
Binding design by Louise E. Jefferson*